THE ARCHITECTURE OF THE JUMPING UNIVERSE

To my daughter
Lily
who jumps

THE ARCHITECTURE OF THE JUMPING UNIVERSE

A POLEMIC: HOW COMPLEXITY SCIENCE IS CHANGING ARCHITECTURE AND CULTURE

CHARLES JENCKS

ACADEMY EDITIONS

REVISED EDITION

ACKNOWLEDGEMENTS:

I started writing the first edition of this friendly polemic soon after Jeffrey Kipnis and I had organized a symposium on Complexity Theory and architecture at the Architectural Association in London. Inevitably I am grateful to the AA for providing the place and pretext to consider the conjunction of these two subjects and, in particular, to Jeffrey for his help and criticism. He has illuminated many aspects of the field in his design and remarks.

Maggie Keswick, my late wife, applied her usual sharp pen to the thickets of my prose, weeded out most of the unfortunate tangles and also supplied some very helpful ideas. I am grateful to her and Maggie Toy, my editor at Academy, for their continuous advice. Rem Koolhaas urged me in several directions which I was at first reluctant to take, but I have followed his guidance on the personal nature of a polemic – even if not as much as he advised. Charlene Spretnak, once again, has steered me through ideas on ecology and our relations with nature, as well as improved my expression in countless ways. I am indebted to her patience over several exasperating hurdles – such as the population bomb – that threatened to knock this text off course. My secretary Valerie Zakian has likewise supplied much patient help and proof-editing.

At Academy Editions this book has been skilfully guided through the rabbit-warren of corrections, layout and editing by Ramona Khambatta, Phil Kirwin and Mario Bettella. I am grateful for their working so efficiently under the pressure of a Christmas deadline. And, for the Second Edition, and another Christmas deadline, Andrea Bettella, Rachel Bean, Alistair Probert and my secretary Sandra Rothwell worked to impossible deadlines with the greatest good humour.

Above all it is Peter Eisenman who has been my most tireless critic and architectural foil. I have known Peter since the late 1960s, a point when we were travelling separate but related paths. Through the years we often discussed architecture, and sparred, but agreed to disagree. Then in the late 1980s, in a surprise to both of us, our paths started to converge. Contemporary science and Complexity Theory, among other issues, yoked us together. Well, here we are, surprisingly good friends – can I say accidentally caused by an emergent property in common? In any case, I am indebted to Peter for many suggestions – his positive comments on such things as 'excess', emergence and superposition – and his negative critique of such things as a 'new aesthetic'. Needless to say I did not take on every change he suggested, but I am inspired by his indefatigable example, his courage and also his unique architecture.

All images are courtesy of the architect, unless otherwise stated: p12 (left) Lockhead Martin Skunk Works (photo: Eric Schulzinger); Thomas Dix pp65, 66-67, 68, 70-71; Bruce Goff p45; Peter Eisenman/Dick Frank pp56, 57; Shigeo Ogawa/Shinkenchiku p57; Zaha Hadid p59; Steven Gerrard p63; Joshua White pp72, 73; E Walvisch p79; Jeffrey Kipnis pp80, 82, 83; Peter Eisenman p84; Peter Cook p97; Prince of Wales' Institute p101; Santiago Calatrava p112; O Koku, K Natori and Renzo Piano pp114, 115; Eamonn O'Mahony pp116, 117; Mike Bluestone p129; ESTO (photos: Jeff Goldberg) p172; L Linder p174; John Gollings pp179, 180; Katsuhisa Kida p181; Joshua White p185.

Front cover illustration: Frank Gehry, The Guggenheim Museum, *Bilbao, Spain, 1993-7.*
Back cover illustration: Ashton Raggart McDougall, RMIT Storey Hall, *Melbourne, Australia, 1994-6.*

First published in Great Britain in 1995, revised edition in 1997 by
ACADEMY EDITIONS

A division of
JOHN WILEY & SONS
Baffins Lane, Chichester
West Sussex PO19 1UD

ISBN: 0-471-97748-9

Other Wiley Editorial Offices
New York • Weinheim • Brisbane • Singapore • Toronto

Printed and bound in Singapore

Contents

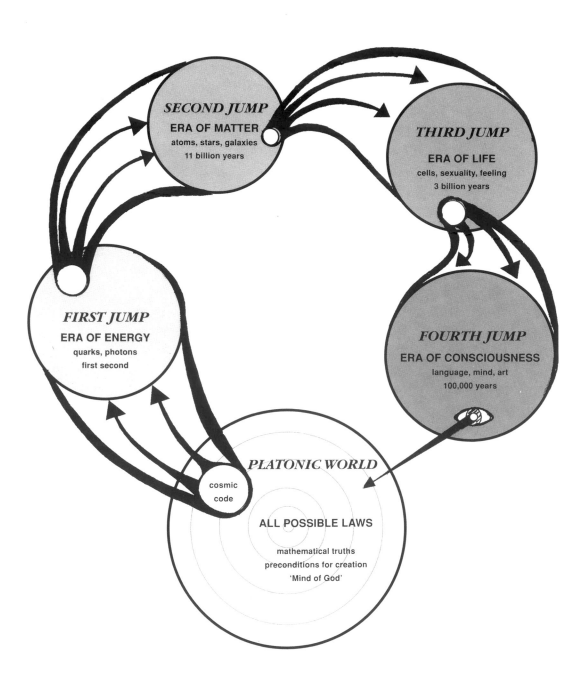

Four Jumps to Consciousness. *Each of the four worlds emerged unpredictably from a small part of its predecessor, and our own world is the first to reflect back on the underlying causes and laws. One part of these laws, the Cosmic Code which scientists are slowly decoding, created the initial inflation badly named the 'Big Bang'. Because new, holistic worlds really do emerge with their own internal laws and being, the reductivist programme of Modern science will only produce partial truths.*

INTRODUCTION: THE JUMPING UNIVERSE

God's not in heaven, the Prince has lost his wife, and all's wrong with the world. For more than fifty years, the complaint has been that society has lost its orientation. But the trouble started earlier; ever since Copernicus displaced man from the center of things, Darwin gave him a family tree of apes from which to swing, and Freud turned his loving soul into an impulse-driven psyche, many have assumed this disorientation to be permanent. Nietzsche, of course, celebrated the death of God because it promoted the freedom and power of future man, superman, and recently Deconstructionists and the Archbishop of Canterbury – to name opposites – have drawn different conclusions from this secular shift. They do, however, agree on one thing: society lacks direction, it is disintegrating into angry fragments. Many post-modernists claim that it is confused because there is no shared philosophy, no 'metanarrative'.

Against this background of dissent and decline is an unnoticed growth. A new world-view has started to spring up. For the first time in the West since the twelfth century we are beginning to construct an all-encompassing story that could unite people of the globe, a metanarrative of the universe and its creation. This is emerging from contemporary science and cosmology, which are again asking the deep questions: Where do we come from? Who are we? How do we fit into an evolving world?

Our recent understanding is quite unique. We are the first generation to know the approximate age of the universe, its likely origin, the main lines of its history, and its fundamental principle of increasing complexity. We are the first to unravel the major laws of its development, and the creativity, beauty and catastrophe they must bring. We are the first to understand our significant place in a single, unfolding process that has lasted some fifteen billion years – and we are the first to celebrate and question these discoveries. In fact, we have a more creative view of nature than either the Christians or Modernists could conceive.

What is this view? It is the unlikely idea – especially surprising to those who thought nature was a machine, or like Darwin, that it evolved gradually – that the universe jumps. As I will show with nonlinearity, catastrophe and emergence theories, nature goes through sudden phase transitions akin to quantum leaps. There are, it is true, continuities and gradual developments, but the basic history of the universe is one of creative, surprising leaps in organization. Traditional religions emphasize constancy, the Modernists with their mechanistic models emphasize predictability, but the cosmos is much more dynamic than either a pre-designed world or a dead machine.

Think how unlikely its history is. In the last fifteen billion years only four, really basic changes have happened. Something badly named the 'Big Bang' created energy, this dynamic pulse partly froze into matter, then matter jumped into life and life gave us sentient creatures and consciousness. Only four main acts (though I will show many lesser ones in Chapter XX). To fully appreciate the strange significance of the four and many leaps, fifteen billion years would need to be collapsed into a two-hour film, giving drama to the sequence of events and the mysteries of emergence.

Why should energy, then matter, arise out of the Cosmic Code? This code is a selection from the possible laws which can cohere into a universe. Might these laws be, as the prophet Isaiah and the cosmologist Stephen Hawking claim, 'thoughts in the mind of God'? Are they finely balanced, even fine-tuned? Or are they just brute contingencies, a matter of very improbable luck – something approaching the odds of a billion billion to one? And then why should they produce insect societies and animals with feelings; why should sentience suddenly emerge from the physical world? Or – the jump which now finds us in mid-air – why should our minds and mathematics be so good at laying bare the Cosmic Code? The facts of each shift are now known and not in dispute, but the explanation remains enigmatic. Each jump is a great mystery and – it now appears, with the theory of emergence itself – our everyday world shows a series of lesser shifts all the time – 'emergencies' as they are sometimes called. The implications of this new world-view are disturbing because they show that violence and mass-extinction are essential parts of evolution. Yet they are also promising, because they suggest we are built, in some fundamental way, into the laws of the universe. We are not, as Modernists and nihilists thought, entirely accidental or alienated from the world.

The main outlines of the universe story I have sketched are now accepted as standard science but this still leaves open the most crucial question: who is to interpret these laws – just scientists and theologians? And what language should they use, what metaphors and art are appropriate to the story? Here, it strikes me, a chronic and depressing problem faces our culture.

Inadequate Science and Religion
Science and religion have been the two principal means we have used to explain ultimate truths, but these traditions have both become inadequate at presenting the significance of recent discoveries. Confronted by the extraordinary truths that have emerged, they both suffer a kind of cultural autism. It is true, as the theologian Thomas Berry says, that science is the longest unbroken meditation on the universe. It is also a progressive meditation, that is, it results in progress and itself shows progress. But scientists may not understand the

wider implications of their theories which must, in the nature of science, be very limited and specialized. Or, just as bad, they may be unable to interpret the implications in larger, cosmic ways, within a broad cultural and spiritual tradition. As I will argue in Part Three, their explanations tend to be adolescent metaphors. Where did the universe come from? A 'Big Bang'. How it will end? 'Big Crunch'. And what constitutes 90 per cent of its basic stuff? 'Machos' and 'wimps'. Much of science, as a tradition, is growing a systematically gray view of the universe, something that trivializes its grandeur. The reason goes to the heart of the modern world-view. Many modern scientists, like Richard Dawkins, think nature is either purposeless (their injunction is 'Don't ask why') or else vicious, that is, built on warfare. They have swallowed the Darwinian world-view and, in turn, have been devoured by it: they end up seeing 'selfish genes' as ultimate truths.

Theologians may also be limited in their outlook since, mostly, they are tied into past beliefs and traditional explanations. They tend, in order to avoid excommunication, to stuff new discoveries into old scriptures. How depressing, how alienating; this traditionalism cuts us off from nature and the unfolding story of the universe. It is true there are some religious teachers who have a deeper vision, one informed by culture and one which articulates our relationship to the cosmos from within. When they distinguish between the benign and hostile aspects, it is possible to identify with some of the more positive cosmic meanings, and to see how we have grown from a small selection of them. Nature may indeed prune itself on warfare, may have a selfish force at work, but its self-organizing drive is deeper, more benign, and it gives an endless bounty of beauty, delight and energy – a giveaway to celebrate.

Thus there are two basic sides to the universe: the selective and self-organizing; and two basic dialogues with nature: the scientific and religious. The former gives us the external laws and the latter the internal ways of relating to nature; or, simply put, objective equations and a poetic projection of our place in the world. But both dialogues have lost their greater vision and become parochial, defensive, lacking in wit, drama, grandeur and surprise (and the new universe story is nothing if not surprising). These two failures would be depressing if they were the only discourses, but where science and religion have been inadequate in interpreting the emergent world-view a fissure has opened up – and an opportunity for others with a different cultural background. Here the artist, architect and writer can enter and construct new territory, lay claim to badly-named realities and create better metaphors and understanding.

I will devote this book largely to others and argue a more general case, but in my own work as a designer in Scotland I have tested some of these premises.

Along with scientists, craftsmen and my late wife Maggie Keswick, I have sought new forms, models and metaphors for the cosmic story, the unfolding universe. Because it is a process and not a static entity, I have called it 'cosmogenesis'. How to present the dynamism of this story? In a spherical model it is shown as an holistic globe spiralling out from a center, like a wave gathering momentum (see p129). However, if presented as a developing, jumping process, it can be seen as an expanding trumpet with thirty leaps marked as steps (see p126). Yet exactly the same narrative can be portrayed in a different metaphor: in a garden terrace the four jumps are dramatized as symmetry breaks in a pattern of grass and pebbles. These end in the leap of consciousness: a growing hedge that will fly over the wall and terrace. Thus three different solutions, all compatible with the standard model of the universe and all alternatives to the metaphor of the Big Bang.

Post-Christian and Post-Modern

Standard science and historical theology are being transformed here in a way that could be called Post-Christian and Post-Modern because it grows out of Christianity and Modernism alike. Modernism itself was a Post-Christian movement, but it was based on a mechanistic science and a view that the universe developed gradually and deterministically. By contrast, the post-modern 'sciences of complexity' explain a more creative world, a picture filled out by many emergent sciences such as fractals, Chaos Theory, nonlinear dynamics and Complexity Theory itself (for an evolutionary chart of these sciences see p124). Taken together they paint an entity that is more like a dynamic organism than a dead machine and one which, like the Christian world-view, has a certain purpose or telos (though not a final teleology).

Charles Jencks, Symmetry Break Terrace, *Scotland, 1995. The four jumps from left to right: (1) burst of energy in straight lines; (2) matter emerges to bend space and time; (3) life emerges from matter, oval shape; (4) consciousness, a hedge, springs out of life and grows.*

What is common to this view of cosmogenesis and the Christian world view? The heart of the Christian faith is the Genesis story that culminates in Christ, a linear, sequential view of history and one, incidentally, which distinguishes it from many other religions. This narrative of history – with its teleological beginning, middle and end – led to the Modernist view of progressive development. Now we may know there is more than one, positive arrow of time – the Second Law of Thermodynamics entails dissolution – but the notion of time as creative and directional has been taken over from both Christians and Modernists to become our new story of cosmogenesis, the universe as self-organizing and growing in certain directions. Paradoxically, it is a story that can be hard to accept, even for its inventors such as Einstein (who so wanted to believe in a static, perfect, eternal universe that he fudged his equations for ten years).

Life of Forms

For artists and architects to portray the new world view with its dynamism and ceaseless fecundity, either new languages of expression must be sought, or previous languages developed further. The life of forms in art is the measure of cosmogenesis. In this sense, an aesthetics of creativity is the last judge of the cosmic process. Of course, 'Make it New' has been a principle of Modernism from Wordsworth to Ezra Pound and 'The Tradition of the New' a cliché since Harold Rosenberg coined the phrase in the 1960s. The newness advocated here, typical of the cosmogenic process, is that of changing DNA or a growing galaxy – one that also keeps a memory of its past. This is the typical creativity of post-modernism, a double-coded creativity that links past, present and future in an inclusive continuum. What are some of its products?

On the large scale, the authors Michael Batty and Paul Longley have identified the new way of thinking about urban life – their book *Fractal Cities*, 1994, described the dynamic, pulsating form of city growth and death. London and Los Angeles are typical fractal cities, star-shaped blobs that seem to flicker and grow along electronic lines of communication. Fly over them at night, or better, get the satellite view, and you can begin to understand the truth of these supple bodies, whose life depends on constant death and renewal through the growth of small businesses. Real cities are quite different from the mechanistic models that Le Corbusier and other Modernists imposed on this process of life and, with the fractal paradigm in mind, planners can now get closer to the fine-grained, subtle growth and work with it.

A new language of form based on fractal design is beginning to permeate our landscape – and skies. The F-117A Stealth Fighter, and its subsequent offspring, were designed to be invisible to radar, and this requirement has generated a series of self-similar forms which reflect radar beams. The result resembles some recent fractal architecture – fractured planes, crystal shapes, forms that catch the light and shadow in brilliant chiaroscuro. This is reminiscent of the crystalline structures that Expressionist architects proposed in the 1920s, but the folded plates have a different rationale and are not designed to resemble crystals: they are generated by computers and new conditions so their form-language is quite different. Toby Russell, who works at a small scale designing bowls and vases, accentuates the same fractured aesthetic by using highly polished surfaces. These reflect the self-similar curves thus multiplying the similarity. But uncanny dark spots, folds and shadows also flicker across the surface, a consequence of the feedback of reflections on reflections.

In his project for an addition to the Victoria & Albert Museum in London, Daniel Libeskind has produced a fractal architecture that jumps out of the ground in a series of six leaps. Six boxes push through each other, part cubes, part rhomboids like the ace of diamonds. The flat, intersecting walls, as calculated by the engineer Cecil Balmond, actually become the structure, allowing column-free interiors, so the crushing shapes have a functional rationale. Generated and proved by computer, these may resemble an ice flow or a Cubist building, but their aesthetic is also somewhat new. It has been mistakenly called Deconstructionist because the forms collide at odd angles, but the form-language is much more unified and self-similar than work in this tradition, and its intentions are not to deconstruct the surrounding environment. Far from it. Libeskind has taken the tiling idea from the extensive collection of tiles at the V&A, he has quoted inscriptions on the existing building as justification – 'Inspiration and Knowledge' (the twin motives I will be emphasizing, of creativity and science) – and he has been led to his overall spiral by the continuous route within the galleries. This culminates in an observation deck.

LEFT: *Lockheed Martin,* F-117A Stealth Fighter. *Fractured planes, a fractal that makes the plane invisible to radar.* RIGHT: *Toby Russell,* Two Aqualine Vases, *London, 1994, silver 370 × 170cm. S-shaped curves reflect back self-similar images to double the fractals.*

Libeskind's post-modern motives, to extend the past in new ways, do not constitute a complete break with history. Rather they are shifts which extend the existing fabric. A set of six fractal shapes at the large scale are supplemented by smaller 'fractiles' at three lesser scales. These self-similar tiles are shaped like an angled L- or V-boot, something not far from the larger rhomboids, so there is a unifying pattern. The L-forms dance over the surface in mirror-image, flips and rotations – standard steps, as shown by the million tiles within the V&A. Yet their colored syncopation also has a new, explosive beat. Past, present and future are equally acknowledged.

Another form-language is growing besides the fractal, an aesthetic based on waves, folds and undulations. Often this form-language is derived, by analogy, from the wave motion that underlies solitons and the quantum world and, perhaps, from Superstrings – those minuscule vibrating units of substance – which underlie the universe itself. Also part of the new repertoire are the twist and warp, characteristic motifs of dramatic change which Catastrophe Theory has illuminated in so many areas. It is no surprise to find these jumping shapes emerging in what might be called Nonlinear Architecture (after nonlinear dynamics, a generic name for the complexity sciences). A new shared language of expression is growing, an aesthetic of undulating movement, of surprising, billowing crystals, fractured planes, and spiralling growth, of wave-forms, twists and folds – a language more in tune with an unfolding, jumping cosmos than the rigid architectures of the past.

In the new sciences and architectures the fundamental idea relates to feedback, self-organizing change, which the computer is well-adapted to portray. Now, as the architects Frank Gehry and Nicholas Grimshaw have shown, we can conceive of curved, dynamic structures as easily as square ones, a warped grid

Daniel Libeskind, proposed addition to the Victoria & Albert Museum, *London, 1996. Six tilted trapezoids spiral through each other and form a new, structurally sound shape. Tiles in V- and L-forms are in different scales and colors – self-similar 'fractiles'.*

as efficiently as a regular one. What's more, as Peter Eisenman has demonstrated, with the computer we can generate architecture which we do not understand beforehand or entirely control, we can grow patterns of nonlinearity – wave-forms that suddenly expand or shrink depending on the feedback.

Such architecture is opposed to, or resists, the mainstream Modern architecture that still dominates the profession, the architecture that grew out of the Newtonian, mechanistic world-view, the architecture that reflects homo economicus and his boring nine-to-five routine. At the end of the day we are seeking another architecture which more adequately reflects the new world-view, the truth that we inhabit a self-organizing universe, more surprising and open-ended than previously imagined. Every being in it, from the atom to the nation to the galaxy, has a quality of self-organization and a degree of free-dom, the ability to reorganize itself through feedback. Even inanimate matter, such as the Red Spot of Jupiter or a hurricane smashing into land, has this quality. If you doubt it, look into yourself, look at the two most important organs in your body, the brain and heart. Each depends on subtle self-organizing rhythms which now can be modelled by the computer; each is balanced in a delicate zone between too much order and too much chaos; each has the organization of what is called 'a strange attractor'. If the brain's rhythms become too ordered, too repetitive, one has a fit; if the heart's rhythms become too irregular, a heart attack. Computer models of a virtual heart show the self-organizing patterns of electrical activity which pulse through it as they move from the zone of delicate balance to chaos, from self-similar rhythms to ar-rhythmia, from healthy complexity to quivering fibrillation. Architects, design-ers, artists – as Ruskin might have urged – look into your heart and study the patterns, they show another aesthetic: the aesthetic of life.

Plan of the Book
The first section of this friendly polemic looks at the general issues of where design is today, what it might represent of importance, and how ideas behind complexity science relate to post-modernism and the past – especially Coleridge's fruitful notion of the transforming powers of imagination. The most controver-sial part of this section – a Cosmic Axiology – contends that value really is in the universe independent of us, and it grows there in greater degrees of com-plexity. Modernists and Christians, especially, will disagree, because they are so used to being told that we are the great exception in nature, that nature in itself is valueless, it knows no good or evil apart from our projections, and that all truth, beauty and goodness lie in the eye of the beholder. I do not expect everyone will come away from this chapter convinced – a polemic, however friendly, states a brief case rather than makes an extended argument.

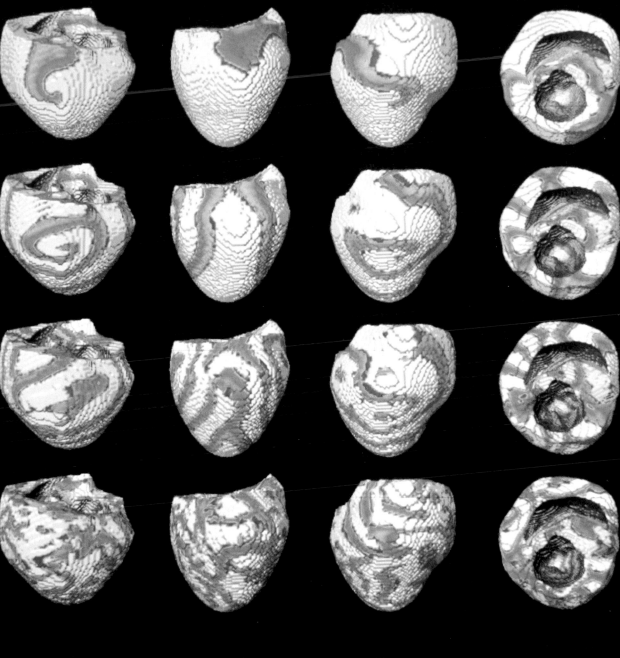

Dr Arun Holden, computer model of a virtual heart, *Leeds University, 1994. Electrical and other complex activities of cells, muscles, etc, are visualized from four sides. Top to bottom shows the movement from a fractal order (health) towards great disorder (fibrillation).*

Part Two looks at the various languages and theories of 'Nonlinear Architecture' – fractals, wave-forms, folded forms and strategies such as superposition – as well as the related movements of Green architecture and 'Organi-tech'.

Part Three raises an historical question: was Modernism, between 1890 and 1920, on the verge of a cosmic and spiritual architecture? Were the early Bauhaus and Le Corbusier motivated by the same ideals as those proffered here before they switched to the Machine Aesthetic and mechanistic view of life? I have become a little more confident of this conjecture since the first edition of this book. I believe there was a spiritual tradition of Modernism in all the arts which was related to contemporary science, but curiously no single monograph has ever pulled all the strands together to prove the point, so the conjecture has to be left open. In any case, I here argue for a cosmogenic architecture adequate to our view of cosmogenesis, and end the second edition with a discussion of buildings that have recently been finished in this emergent tradition.

The basic question that has to be asked is: why is this new paradigm important? Is the Nonlinear Architecture somehow superior, closer to nature and our understanding of the cosmos than old Modernism? Is it more sensuous, functional, livable and closer to the aesthetic codes built into perception? Has it supplanted the tradition from which it has grown (Neo-Expressionist and Deconstructionist architecture)? Can it produce a more subtle urban order than the functional planning of Modernism; will its close-grained urban fabric, its fractal order, be more conducive to economic growth and urban coherence? Finally, will we recognize in its forms the basic truths that the complexity sciences are revealing? Will it capture the truths of a jumping universe?

Charles Jencks, Fractal Desk, *Scotland, 1995.*

16

PART ONE

SIMPLICITY AND COMPLEXITY

Complexity arising from simple contrary requirements (museum, observatory deck, restaurant, centralized space) and different languages of architecture (industrial, vernacular, classical). Aldo Rossi, Bonnefanten Museum, *Maastricht, 1995.*

I
FIASCO IN BERLIN

In the West there is a crisis in architecture that reveals a crisis in culture and the way we live today. Western society is confused, politicians lack direction and architects, who are meant to crystallize the noblest aspirations of an age, are at a loss as to what to represent. Architecture reflects society, it is often said, and the mirror it holds up today is fractured with a thousand different images, some of them very exciting, many of them disturbing, but all of them marginalized. Our age has lost its unifying ethos, its Christian roots, the modernist beliefs in progress, Marxism, socialism, even triumphant capitalism. The era of 'isms' replacing religions has been superseded, and even the avant-garde hangs its head.

What is to be done? The question cannot even be asked without an ironic nod at history, for how many times was it asked in the nineteenth century, only to be answered at a later date with unintended results – such as the Russian Revolution. To ask it again today is to invite sceptical dismissal. But consider a recent competition in Berlin – the center of the new Europe – and what it tells us about the condition of culture today. In February 1993 a jury of twenty-three handpicked architects and experts waded through 835 entries from around the world for an exceptionally auspicious site and program, undoubtedly the most significant in the world today. In the early 1940s the Spreebogen area, where the Spree River bends in Berlin, had been cleared by Adolf Hitler, in preparation for a glorious city, Germania, which he foresaw as 'the capital of the world'. Since then many sites in the city have been opened by bomb damage and the destruction of the Berlin Wall, but none is so huge and symbolically potent as this one. It was to be the focus for the Third Reich, empire of a thousand years, and Albert Speer had designed a helmeted dome sixteen times the size of St Peter's to impress on the visitor that a new secular religion had superseded that of the Caesars and Popes.

In the end, all that Hitler left was a *tabula rasa*, a burnt-out, domeless Reichstag and the biggest challenge to architecture since London burned in the seventeenth century. What should be done with the dividing line between the former East and West Berlin, between, in other words, the two dominant paradigms of modernity – communism and capitalism ?

How should one represent the new prime symbols of power? How, in a country embarrassed by Prussian and Nazi classicism, should one treat the Reichstag – the 'Imperial Diet'? Rebuild the old dome, and recall fascism? Have the engineer Santiago Calatrava build his ovoid, known affectionately as the 'egg cup'? Or have Norman Foster build his sheltering canopy known as 'the petrol station' (which may, actually, allow people to watch the deliberations of parliament)?

Perhaps, as competitors suggested, one should cut the Reichstag in two, cover it with a web, or wrap it like a Christo package. And what to do with the new democratic seat of government, the Bundesrat?

The Spreebogen competition provided an opportunity to address the basic issues of our time – politically, spiritually, ecologically – with an architecture that symbolized a new dawn. What was the result? According to one writer:

> . . . grids, semi-circles, skyscrapers, groups of small low buildings, polite classically inspired schemes, arrangements of oddly angled shards, a few nihilistic and apocalyptic entries, several anthropomorphic designs, and one that looked like a serving of eggs and vegetables.[1]

No bananas, no cocktail sticks? We have seen such collections many times recently, especially in World Fairs – so, apparently, had the jurors:

> Out of all the drawings and models that had taken months to prepare and cost architecture firms around the world enormous sums, there was nothing inspiring, no brilliant or distinctive proposal that would provide an image for the new Germany or the city of Berlin . . . [The jurors] fretted about the dismal showing by their colleagues and the state of the profession in their respective countries. There was talk about awarding no prize at all . . . Appropriate architectural imagery is still an open question.[2]

Yes, it is an open question: in what style are we to build? Or, more exactly, what is architecture *to be about* in an age of confusion? What is the credible belief system to represent? What the content beyond our anthropomorphic concerns?

For many architects and their modernist public, this is a dead issue, a nineteenth-century question decided long ago. 'Architecture is about process, Stupid. It's about the *making* of architecture – function, technology, construction,

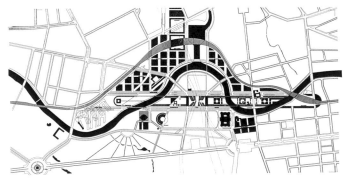

Axel Schultes, Winning Spreebogen Design, *Berlin, 1993, a central spine of government buildings in a severe Prussian Functionalist block-geometry.*

light, space, and all the architectural means used in building. Nothing else.' As the Modern poet Archibald MacLeish said, 'A poem doesn't mean, it just is'. Or, as Clement Greenberg summarized the Modern impulse in all the arts, it is about aesthetic autonomy, the uniqueness of each process. Thus painting is about two-dimensionality, sculpture about three-dimensionality, architecture about a bit more, and so on. I exaggerate, but not much. Such formulas may have convinced a small band of abstractionists or materialists and, on a positive note, reduced the amount of kitsch produced in the twentieth century – an aim of Greenberg – but the reduction of art and poetry to a creative investigation of means could not satisfy anyone for very long. Both artists and public soon understood the fallacy (although still addicted to the practice).

So again the question presses itself upon us, especially when we redesign a center of Western civilization and are prepared to pay $4 million just for architects to compete with an answer. Just what is civic life today – what is its *shared* content? Architects, more than any other profession, are paid to worry about such questions for the obvious reason that their art is so necessarily public. Writers, TV directors and politicians may fret about the momentary meaning of their products, but these come and go with the weather and do not, like architecture, sit around for decades, occupying space and preventing other choices. There can be an infinity of *Hamlets* on CD which take up no space, and cause no pollution, but there is room for only one Kremlin, one Reichstag, one Vatican, one Rome. If building takes possession of space then, as a city fills up, architecture, as in chess, becomes an End Game with only a few moves left. So choices about style and content matter as in no other art. They remind us who we are and to what we aspire; they take the temperature of culture. It has a fever.

For one short period of time, after the First World War and for the next few years, Modern architects addressed such large issues directly. These are the convictions of Walter Gropius at the time he founded the Bauhaus, in 1919:

What is architecture? The crystalline expression of man's noblest thoughts, his ardour, his humanity, his faith, his religion! That it once *was*! But who of those living at this time, cursed as it is with functionalism, does still understand the all embracing and cheering nature of architecture . . . The grey, empty, obtuse stupidities in which we live and work will bear humiliating testimony to the spiritual abyss into which our generation has slid . . . Ideas perish as soon as they are compromised . . . Build in fantasy without regard for technical difficulties. To have the gift of imagination is more important than all technology, which always adapts itself to man's creative will.[3]

What a polemic, and how strange, coming from Gropius. ' . . . this time, cursed as it is with functionalism!' Yes, the man who was soon to become an apostle of functionalism proclaimed that one should 'build in fantasy'. One has to make allowances for the after-effects of a ravaging war – and a concomitant Expressionism in reaction to it – but what is also notable about this proclamation is the way it identifies architecture with a cultural temperament cursed by industrialization and bereft of artistic direction. Architecture expresses passion, religion, and noble thought. Its basic motivations cannot be put any more succinctly.

Today the same point may be put as a question about what we build – shopping malls rather than agorac, Disneylands rather than cathedrals. Put another way it is a question of style and content – right angles rather than undulating architecture, I-beams rather than organic details, and habitual rather than emergent structures. To ask the embarrassing question, 'what style and content shall we build?' implies we have choice, at least as much as the entrants to the 1993 Berlin competition. In times of fast change, such questions are asked, while in peaceful times, people are confident with the reigning approach.

Curiously, we live today in a conflicted time of both accelerated change *and* business-as-usual, a time of both transformation and stagnation. This book is addressed to those who want to change the conceptual direction of architecture and forge a larger cultural change. Of course it would be silly, after so much twentieth-century evidence to the contrary, to think that architects could change society. They are relatively powerless compared to politicians, developers, journalists, and businessmen. They can only tinker with ecological and population problems set by others. They do, however, have one power that no other profession enjoys: they have some control of the architectural language and the messages sent. A single building can celebrate a better world or signify a change in direction. It has the power to engage the imagination and symbolize the basic truths of the universe. Man is not the measure of all things – the emergent cosmos is. We are beginning to know some of her predispositions, but the question is: can we build a shared culture on them?

Lyonel Feininger, Cathedral of the Future, *Bauhaus Proclamation, woodcut, 1919.*

II
SHARED LANGUAGE AND COSMIC VALUES

As I have said, the world view which has grown along with contemporary science reveals a fundamentally creative universe – open, dynamic, surprising; and active, not passive. When we look at the heavens, our eyes deceive us, just as the flat-earthers were fooled by their view of a flat horizon five hundred years ago. The stars and galaxies seem static, eternal, or moving slowly in deterministic patterns, becoming the background stage on which we move. But if we could speed up the sequence, we would see how dramatic and unpredictable this background really is – an actor, director, script and stage all at once. Moreover, it is a unified universe, a single unfolding event of which we are an embedded part, a narrative of highly dangerous and fine-tuned events, something more like a detective thriller with many crimes and last-minute escapes than the impersonal account of astronomy textbooks. We are only just beginning to decipher the plot and figure out the Cosmic Code, as Heinz Pagels puts it. The laws of nature are written in subtle languages, many of them counter-intuitive, but a shared narrative has indeed emerged, which I will discuss in Chapter XX. It shows that the exploding universe continuously reaches higher levels of organization, and that we have to adapt to, or learn about, these new levels as we co-evolve with them. If this plot shows the earth co-evolving with our knowledge and civilization, then one story we are involved in is a participatory-detective-romance where the murderer is all around and closing in: the population bomb.

There are many different takes on this plot, equally worthy of architectural representation, and they concern the shift from the view of a static cosmos to a creative cosmogenesis. Characteristically, architecture represents this unfolding process in two ways: by signifying aspects of the changing and growing world directly (its laws, seasons and qualities) and by reflecting them abstractly, in new languages of architecture (or inventive moves in an old language).

Both types of creative change constitute its spiritual function, a role which has gone largely unremarked for seventy years. Before he died in 1989, the English art critic Peter Fuller foresaw some of the connections between a new science and a new spiritual art. In his last book, *Theoria, Art and the Absence of Grace*, he summarizes his hopes for a new, shared, symbolic language of form, something that we both understood as essential for the Post-Modern agenda:

> In the post-modern age, science is rediscovering the aesthetic and spiritual meanings of nature – and Ruskin's dream of a natural theology without God is becoming a reality. [4]

Indeed part of this is true: the Post-Modern sciences of complexity – from quantum physics to chaos science – *are* rediscovering aesthetic and spiritual meanings of nature; meanings that were denied by modernity. The more we discover via these new sciences, the more we find our connectedness to a creative and mysterious universe. On the large scale it is mysterious in the way it leapt suddenly from an energy state to a material one, and awe-inspiring when it jumped into life. But any of its jumps, its runaway growths or sudden crashes, show an unpredictable and extraordinary emergence of something new. The same abrupt creativity is possible for any self-organizing individuals within it.

If the implications are spiritual, there is nevertheless a point that can be questioned. Do they lead to Ruskin's and Fuller's dream of 'a natural theology without God'? Fuller might better have said, at least, 'a natural atheology without God'. You can't have your Theos and eat Him too. Divinity needs to be redefined away from the patriarchical 'Theos' towards a much broader notion of creativity in the cosmos, in which case it will not be 'theology' at stake but, instead, a 'new spirituality without a male god in human image'. This Post-Christian idea returns religion to its much older role, that which it had 30,000 years ago in such places as Lascaux. The older, more mature notion of divinity was generative. Instead of making external products, as does a craftsman, or giving commands over a group, like a sergeant, sacred models favoured those beings that create from within: the goddess or animal or nature as a whole. These became pregnant, expanded and suddenly gave birth.

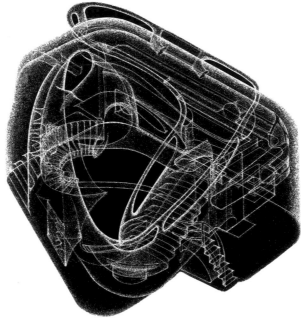

Ushida Findlay Partnership, Truss Wall House, *Machida, Tokyo, 1993, biomorphic, transparent layering of the organs of a house.*

Just before he died tragically in a car crash, Fuller and I had several discussions about where Post-Modernism was going. He was a brilliant and outspoken polemicist, a latter-day Pugin who loved to caricature an opponent and score points in order to further his own cause. He once tarred me with the brush of Disney-kitsch – at a Tate Gallery symposium organized on the subject of one of my books. His methods *were* often bigoted and he loved a nasty swipe; but he also had the courage to speak his mind and go against the mainstream of the art market and the prevailing Modernist orthodoxy. We often disagreed in public, but we both felt strongly that architecture should seek 'a shared symbolic order of the kind that religion provides' and an 'imaginative, yet secular, response to nature herself'. Sadly, in *Theoria*, his one reference to these debates, he shows the typical distortion of an adversarial position. I bring it up here because it bears directly on a central issue of this book: the way we often confuse two necessary but different things – values, and the language in which they are expressed. He writes:

> Post-Modernism knows no commitments: it takes up what one of its leading exponents, Charles Jencks, once called a 'situational position', in which 'no code is inherently better than any other'. The west front of Wells Cathedral, the Parthenon pediment, the plastic and neon signs of Caesar's palace etc . . . are all equally 'interesting'.[5]

In the passage to which he refers, I was talking about codes or architectural languages, not values or the content they expressed. I was defending the relativism of *languages*: German is as 'good' as English; Classical is as 'good' as Gothic architecture; any spoken or natural language that has developed across time is as 'good' as any other. I was not saying that what was said in the language, or the quality of expression, was equal in value. The morality of the architect lies partly in acknowledging the local language when building, in not speaking a totally foreign tongue. Modern architecture went wrong when it imposed a professional language on all locales; hence my call for a double-coding of elite *and* contextual languages – a definition, and one of the moral points, of Post-Modernism that remains valid today.

Yet there is truth in Fuller's distortion of what I meant, if it is applied to 'deconstructive Post-Modernism', for this tradition does urge us towards an absolute relativity. Complete relativism, the idea that all values are the same – or worse, meaningless – is pervasive in our culture and reinforced by the consumer society. It also develops directly from modern nihilism and the philosophies of empiricism, which insisted that values do not exist in the universe, but are mere projections, or social constructions of different societies. Few people probably believe in this absolute relativism, but the combined action of advertisement, the electronic simulation of virtually everything, and a philosophy of mechanism have, together, created a general mood of nihilism. In addition, such deconstructivists as Jean-Francois Lyotard have written that all 'metanarratives' (or stories of science, religion, and progress) have lost their credibility.

By contrast, the tradition of Post-Modernism to which I belong – called variously 'restructive', 'constructive' or 'ecological' – contends that metanarratives have not ended but, rather, have become contested, and are seen now in their plurality.[6] It is this, not nihilism or absolute relativism, that is the big shift in our time: a movement towards the fullness of different meanings and diverse ways of life, continuously created by an expanding universe. If plural meanings did not exist we – or any species that can feel and think – would soon invent them. Cosmic values, as I will argue, precede and are mirrored by aesthetic and social values. Truth, beauty, and morality are not, *pace* so much recent Western philosophy, just in the eye of the beholder.

Given this position, in agreement with Peter Fuller's philosophy, it is sad that we could never iron out our differences. We both wanted this and had planned it but, just at the height of his powers, and at the moment when he had formulated the idea of a new spiritual art based on a possibly shared language of natural symbolism, he died. It is also sad and ironic that, in the one place I refer to him in my own writings, it is precisely to agree that 'distinctions of value can be defined objectively' – that is, as the new sciences of complexity reveal, quality *really is* in the world out there, and in ourselves. They are not just in cultural codes and the eye of the observer, but built into the cosmic codes which generate the universe.

Fractal Code of bifurcations generates a tree of self-similarity.

III
COMPLEXITY IN ARCHITECTURE AND URBANISM

Before I illustrate some ways architecture can embody cosmological values, I should point out a possible point of confusion and a curious historical truth. There are really *two* complexity theories: the architectural and the scientific (what I will call Complexity One and Complexity Two). Each starts its recent history in the early 1960s. They may have influenced each other and grown together, but they are separate enough to deserve separate treatment.

In the late 1950s, the sociologist Herbert Gans showed that the wealth and power of any large city was partly dependent on a series of 'urban villages' that were hidden from view: the complexity of different ways of life, ethnic groups, and skilled minorities that were obscured by the dominant culture. Following Gans, and learning from his ideas, Jane Jacobs wrote one of the important foundation manifestoes of Post-Modernism, *The Death and Life of Great American Cities* (1961). In this polemic, she attacked the Modernist notion that a city could be divided functionally into purified parts, the zoning ideas of Le Corbusier that had helped destroy so many great American cities. At the end of her book, in a chapter titled 'The Kind of Problem a City Is', she makes distinctions that are now canonic in Complexity Theory in science.

A city is *not* particularly a question of functional zoning, or dividing areas up into the 'five functions' – 'living, working, circulating, recreating, governing' – or 'simplicity'. Nor, as she writes, is it particularly a question of 'disorganized complexity' (complete randomness). Both of these processes characterized Modern science, from Newton to the development of statistics.

Rather, she insists, a city is 'a problem of organized complexity' – the organization of many different functions, some small, some large – like those with which the life sciences deal. And this is her point: a city is fundamentally a living organism with complex interlinkages and holistic behaviour. To mention a concept we will find again and again in Complexity Two: like a beehive or ant colony, it is a superorganism with nonlinear, *emergent* properties.

Robert Venturi's *Complexity and Contradiction* (1966), the second important manifesto of Post-Modern architecture and urbanism, also absorbs lessons from the new complexity sciences. He quotes the psychologist and computer-scientist Herbert Simon, and was no doubt aware of cybernetics. His main drift, however, is aesthetic: for him, complexity represents a psychological and social advance over simplicity, an evolution of culture and urbanism to cope with contradictory problems such as the conflict between the inside and outside pressures on a building. He illustrates the work of Mannerist architects, and Borromini and

ABOVE: Francesco Borromini, Oratory of St Philip Neri, *Rome 1637-40. Complex urban requirements lead to an architecture of contradiction. The addition to the left of a grand, stone church led Borromini to this asymmetrical symmetry and a more modest, brick material. The outside contradicts the inside asymmetry; the main entrance is not in the middle but to the right; the concave curves are countered by the concave center, the triangular pediment by semi-circles and the facade is a superposition on a flat substructure; BELOW: Robert Venturi and Denise Scott Brown,* Sainsbury Wing, National Gallery, *London, 1985-91. A series of contradictions between white Classicism, black Modernism and opposing requirements make this small structure a gem of complexity.*

Lutyens, to bring out the superiority of a complex view of the world over a simple one. He also borrows from literary criticism – ideas from Cleanth Brooks and TS Eliot – to make the same point. Here he quotes from August Heckscher:

> The movement from a view of life as essentially simple and orderly to a view of life as complex and ironic is what every individual passes through in becoming mature. But certain epochs encourage this development; in them the paradoxical or dramatic outlook colors the whole intellectual scene . . . Amid simplicity and order rationalism is born, but rationalism proves inadequate in any period of upheaval. Then equilibrium must be created out of opposites. Such inner peace as men gain must represent a tension among contradictions and uncertainties . . . A feeling for paradox allows seemingly dissimilar things to exist side by side, their very incongruity suggesting a kind of truth.[8]

The addition to London's National Gallery illustrates this maturity and inclusive complexity. The building mediates between opposite pressures for which there is no simple solution or single style. It handles the requirements of mass tourism (the entry of three million back-packers per year) *and* stately art appreciation. It engages with the three different adjacent contexts it has to fit into *and* the interior requirements. It does this with two main languages: a new classicism *and* Miesian Modernism. Venturi's book was titled 'Complexity *and* Contradiction' because it uncovered the basic oppositional system between architecture and urbanism, fundamental conflicts which have to be faced, not suppressed.

Several of the most important conflicting forces are represented and fight it out, symphonically, on the five facades. And yet the building still has, as he says it should, 'an obligation towards the difficult whole'. The five different facades still hang together, still form what is called in classical language 'an Order' as they are transformed around each corner. A 'self similarity' – the notion elaborated by the science of fractals – is present, if not invoked.

Venturi's was the first stage of complexity in architecture: complexity as the collage of pre-existing, well-known solutions; complexity as the manipulation of classicism, Modernism, or any familiar ground. But it is more involved with the juxtaposition of static, pre-existing elements than the emergence of surprising new wholes. It is towards the second type – complexity as emergence – that we shall concentrate upon, the scientific development of the idea and the main focus of this book.

IV
COMPLEXITY SCIENCE: THE HEART OF POST-MODERNISM

In 1963 the MIT meteorologist, Edward Lorenz, when trying to work out weather prediction on a computer, inadvertently discovered the basic reality in nature known as deterministic chaos, or *sensitivity to initial conditions*. He found that, because of positive feedback, very small differences of force are amplified into large ones, bringing into play the Butterfly Effect: the insignificant flapping of a butterfly's wings in Singapore is magnified eventually into a hurricane in Florida. Of course many other effects smooth out such disturbances, but in principle – in the weather and other nonlinear systems – there is always some Butterfly Effect.

From this point Lorenz went on to define the repetitive nature of these differences and formulated what came to be known as *strange attractors*; the way chaotic systems may nevertheless have 'limit cycles', maxima and minima, which fluctuate about an area. Temperature and rain fluctuations over a year in New York, for instance, will be pulled towards a strange attractor. The weather has, since Lorenz's formulations, been an important model for Post-Modernists; as important as the clock and orrery were for Newton and the Modernists. Like Fuzzy Logic, the weather is usually a mixture of changeable qualities which can only be approximated.

If this seems a strange exemplar, then for similar reasons the architect, Peter Eisenman, has adopted an even more bizarre standard of thought: the slime mould. This living organism has the extraordinary capacity to exist as both a slimy whole when under threat or hungry, and as set of individual parts when happy or satiated. It can break up and reform, like a good thought, sometimes acting like the selfish, privatized consumer off on a summer holiday, and at other times like a good citizen of the Communist Collective of All Slimes. Like the weather it too is approximate, slithery, supple and self-organizing: indeed all organisms appear to be organized by internal strange attractors.

After Lorenz's discoveries, the computer scientist Benoit Mandelbrot added the notions of *fractals* (fractional dimensions, fractures) to the emergent sciences of complexity and, by the mid 70s, among a small group of scientists, a new view of nature started to emerge. The universe was understood to be fundamentally dynamic, self-organizing on ever higher and higher levels. Inevitably this thinking had many similarities to world views of the past: to those of Buddhism, Taoism, the Romantics and to the cosmological philosophies of Alfred North Whitehead, Eric H Jantsch and others – but all of these had been marginalized by western Modernism.

In the mid 70s, however, realization dawned among a few scientists and philosophers that the cosmos had more *nonlinearity* in it than linearity gathered strength. It became clear that the universe was more like a cloud than a clock, more like a growing fern than a Euclidean structure. Even the eminent rationalist philosopher Karl Popper started to write pregnantly of clouds.

 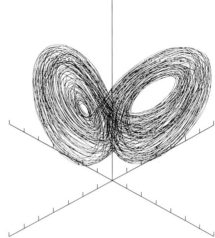

Eighteenth-century orrery *versus twentieth-century* strange attractor. *The difference in world view, implied by each, is instructive. For Newton and the Modernists, nature was as predictable as this teaching model, and the planets and moons followed their deterministic path as they were cranked around their orbits by God or, here, a small lever. For the Post-Modernists the strange attractor – here the one Edward Lorenz discovered – is a much better model of nature: the weather is always self-similar, but never exactly repeating. It is pulled by holistic interactions of pressure, temperature and other factors towards two attractors, two 'eyes', and limited by this chaotic attractor. The continuous holistic interactions 'fold' the recurring shapes towards each other – always varying, always similar. We now know the universe is much more a chaotic attractor than a deterministic mechanism.*

V
DEMONIZING MODERNISM

With clouds replacing clocks, a revolution in thinking was under way, that can best be understood by opposing it to the dominant world view, by contrasting the Post-Modern sciences of complexity with the Modern sciences of simplicity. To bring out the contrast I will reduce Modernism to a few propositions of reductivism – an appropriate oversimplification since this paradigm is itself so reductivist. It continuously demonizes an 'other', so it is reasonable to return its own medicine.

Modern science – that of Galileo, Descartes, Newton and Darwin – grew out of, and depended upon, the Christian world view and a rational, 'designer' God. It is a point long recognized that Modern science developed only once, and in the West, because Christianity placed such emphasis on the reasonable way the universe was made: with laws, invented by a single law-giver, waiting to be discovered. As depicted in paintings and literature, it was decided on and crafted by a male God 'out there, and up there' somewhere in the cosmos over our heads. The thirteenth-century illustration of 'God the architect', taken from a Moralized Bible, shows this external architect separating the four elements from chaos, imposing a Euclidean order on the deep (as *Genesis* might have it). The male architect making something – the cosmos – might be contrasted with a self-birthing process as an external versus internal action, an alienating versus involving process. The former disconnects the universe and us from the basic creative powers of invention, fecundity, gestation and change.

From such an external, Deist God springs the rational clockwork world. It is He who has perfectly crafted its equations, wound it up and, sadly for those who wish He were still concerned, let it go. Here was fabricated the linear world of determinism. Under Newtonism, it turns into three more of the great 'isms of Modernism' – reductivism, mechanism, and materialism (which, because they are still so dominant, you will hear damned, like a refrain, throughout this book).

The Modernist view of life ultimately led to the killing fields of mechanized warfare and, on a trivial but fashionable level, the moronic phrases of Andy Warhol: 'I want to be a machine . . . machines have fewer problems'. It also led the Behaviourist BF Skinner to educate his daughter in a Skinner Box, and to Madonna's bragging song, 'Material Girl'. It led to the totalitarian state – a Modernist version of traditional dictatorship – and far too many idiocies of conditioning to mention. Mass-produced advertisement, intended to condition us as if we were robots, is unthinkable without the four great 'isms of Modernism'.

But what of the architectural and artistic languages derived from the Modern paradigm? 'Saint' Newton's world (for he was literally canonized in textbooks, buildings and poems throughout Europe) was built just as the French architect Etienne-Louis Boullée designed his cenotaph: in monumental Platonic solids and Phileben forms. These are the squares, cylinders, triangles and perfect forms that even the nature-loving Cézanne would say, two hundred years later, under-lay all nature. Yes, even Cézanne, who studied and sketched every day in the voluptuous hills of Provence, was taken in by this square view of nature. From Ledoux to Le Corbusier (as one book is titled) is a small step from Euclidean formalism to 'the masterly, correct and magnificent play of sunlight over pure forms – Phileban forms'. And from Le Corbusier to Norman Foster it is a mere half-step, the two-step, the same mechanical ballet, the same deterministic world view with the same materialism, even if it is a spiritual materialism devoutly worshipped and detailed (as it is with Foster and other High-Tech architects).

In some lights this religious-mechanical architecture can be beautiful; but there are clearly negative consequences to other parts of the Modern paradigm. According to the sociologist Zygmunt Bauman (*Modernity and the Holocaust*, 1989) this determinist world view also led – indirectly, I should emphasize – to the Holocaust. It is possible that it also led to the collaboration of Mies van der Rohe with the Nazis, the compromise of Le Corbusier with Mussolini and Petain, and of Terragni with the Fascists. It could also explain why Walter Gropius was led to write compromising letters to Goebbels defending the 'Germanness' of Modern architecture, and then design a very compromised classical-modern structure for Hitler's Reichsbank. Many Modernists, *in spite of a hatred for fascism*, ended up complicit with the totalitarian currents of the 1930s.

FROM LEFT TO RIGHT: God the architect, *from a* Moralized Bible, *France, fourteenth century; Otto von Spreckelsen,* La Grande Arche de la Défense, *Paris, 1982-89. Monomaniacalmegabuild; Toyo Ito,* White Noise, *Japan Exhibition, Victoria and Albert Museum, London, 1992, liquid crystal architecture – information glut destroys narrative.*

Why did they do this? There were many reasons, among them a common will-to-power and, as Bauman makes clear, the fatal connection between instrumentalist reason and the rationalist philosophy: 'the ends justify the means', and rational cost-benefit analysis. Of course, coercion and fear played great roles too, but basically the deterministic world view tends to make one fatalistic with respect to the power structure.

So much for the virtues of determinism; what about the machine aesthetic and the machine idolatry of Modernism? A mechanistic world view, quite obviously, leads to battery-hatch housing and concentration camp planning. I need not prove this: Pruitt-Igoes, Sarcelles, and just about all the high-rise fortresses that surround every modern city from New York to Moscow, unfortunately, nail in the point. Here the problems are so obvious – and have been attacked since before Prince Charles was even conceived – that we might confine our diagnosis to the more arcane subject of naming the major architectural diseases caused by the mechanistic world view.

There is the most virulent malady caused by mass-production – 'monothematatis' – in which a good theme is repeated so often it is done to death. Machine production also brings on 'archiamnesia' in which neighborhoods are levelled and all traces of the past are purged. This serves as a perfect excuse for justifying outrageous monuments: inappropriate symbols stolen from the past, such as IM Pei's Paris pyramid – a clear example of 'blasphemesis'. Further diseases are 'malaproptosis' and the quite horribly-sounding 'monomaniacalmegabuild', which is painfully evident near the heart of Paris, in an area called La Défense. La defense? There is no defense against *homo economicus* multiplying like a cancer. 'Monomaniacalmegabuild!'

These terms, alas, have yet to be accepted by the medical establishment.

The Late-Modern version of this world-view exaggerates certain of the inherent ideas. Reductivism becomes the extreme simplicity of the minimalists: the 'less is more' of Mies becomes 'more of less is even more' of Foster. Mies, in his spiritually ascetic mode, extolled the virtues of 'almost nothing' – and this limit condition has been reached in the Late-Modern silences of John Cage's music, and the fashionable emphasis on the 'presence of the absence'. Or else the logic can go the other way to a kind of 'white noise': the absolute saturation of information in Toyo Ito's liquid crystal architecture, or the extreme and violent complications of Lebbeus Woods' and Coop Himmelblau's work. Extreme reductivism, silence, is like extreme complication, noise, since both destroy narrative and organization; the former by a dearth of information, the latter by a glut.

The whole point of the Information Age – usually missed by those in its technical thrall – is the quality, not the quantity of information.

VI

HOW MUCH COMPLEXITY? – A COSMIC AXIOLOGY

Having criticized Modernism and its reductionism, I should qualify the general point. There are some positive aspects of Modernity, including those I have mentioned in the introduction, such as its fight for universal rights and a progressive technology.

There are different contexts where extreme simplicity is called for, including political rhetoric, advertisement and the formulation of a law of nature – for instance Einstein's general theory of relativity. All laws are simple compressions of complex behaviour; that is, the discovery of simple rules, algorithms, and descriptions behind what appear to be unrelated phenomena. Indeed, the point of a law of nature is to reduce complexity to simplicity. Simplicity can also be suitable for portraying the sublime and heroic. Norman Foster's Stanstead Airport appropriately reduces architecture to a grand space of clear transition and floating structures, a single awesome and beautiful statement.

However, most building tasks which involve many conflicting functions, different taste-cultures and new and old fabric, demand a more complex response. The same is true of most art and rhetorical forms: the novel and film thrive on complicated twists in plot and conflicting characters and cultures. As the number of competing elements increases in a work of art or architecture, it obviously must move from a simple integrated statement to something more complex. How can we judge these different types of work?

As a first approximation, imagine a continuum of typical Modern works of art, starting with the simplest and progressing to the most complicated. We might commence around 1918 with Malevich's canvas *White on White*, or Rodchenko's *Black on Black*; canvasses that are maximally simple, regular, and ordered – and, if we want to guess the whole from the part, most predictable. I should emphasize that for the moment I am concerned here only with those works as formal, not signifying, systems.

Jump to the other Modern extreme, Jackson Pollock's free-form Action Paintings of the late 1940s, and we find maximum randomness: the squiggles, swirls, blotches, and spatters that recorded his activity as he danced over a canvas on the floor. While both extremes look absolute, their art consists in being a little less so: faint white and black forms can be barely discerned in the former cases, and the apparently chaotic squiggles have *some* order in the latter. Nevertheless, they can symbolize here the extremes to which Modern artists are pushed. What are the pressures that push them? Negatively, a commercial art market demanding the Shock of the New; cultural norms of Modernism demanding 'otherness', and 'difficulty' for its own sake (or the sake of the art coterie). Positively, in some cases, a search for the conceptual and spiritual in art.

Whatever the motives, a totally ordered *and* disordered art, a completely regular *and* chaotic environment, are naturally produced by our economic-cultural system. What we want today in architecture and art is something between and, as we will see, at right angles to these extremes.

As a second approximation to judging the continuum from order to disorder, imagine our line pulled up in the middle of the work of art to form a pyramid, with the vertical axis measuring the degree of structure, or organization.

Again, simple ordered things are to the left – clichés, slogans, one-liners – and to the far right such complicated things as dictionaries, encyclopedias, and a list of the one trillion galaxies recently discovered. Between these extremes, and raised above them on the slope of the curve, are poetic works, the *Summa Theologica* of Thomas Aquinas (an encyclopedia with a purpose), and *Hamlet*. These have some order and some randomness, some simplicity and some complication, some predictability and some entropy (a measure of disorder): they are all somewhere in the middle between the two extremes, *and* they have internal structure.

Many critics contend that the latter group of works is inherently more valuable and long-lasting than either of the former extremes. They will be reinterpreted again and again by each new audience precisely because this richer organization leads to varied but coherent readings. Shall I put it dogmatically? One index of the most valuable art is its invitation to the imagination: it can be legitimately read the most number of ways. How many ways can you decipher the typical 'dumb box' found in every downtown area of a city, the Modern curtain-walled office of glass and steel?

By contrast, can we measure well-organized works; the precise way complexity is more structured than either simplicity or complication? In some fields, yes. A recently developed mathematics, called 'algorithmic complexity theory', purports to measure the degree of biological structure – that is the *quality* of organization – of one organism versus another, by giving explicit numerical value to its relative progress, or the complexity of its development.[9]

The same method applied to art or literature would measure this quality by comparing it to the cost of a computer program that it would take to reproduce a facsimile of the work. In the case of the nearly black canvas, *Black on Black*, or the one covered with nearly random squiggles, that of Jackson Pollock, the length of computer description is fairly short. In the case of *Hamlet*, or any other work rich in organization, it is no shorter than the work itself. Thus the length of a 'proper description' by computer or algorithm measures the formal quality of the work. But I put quotes around 'proper description' to show that the particu-

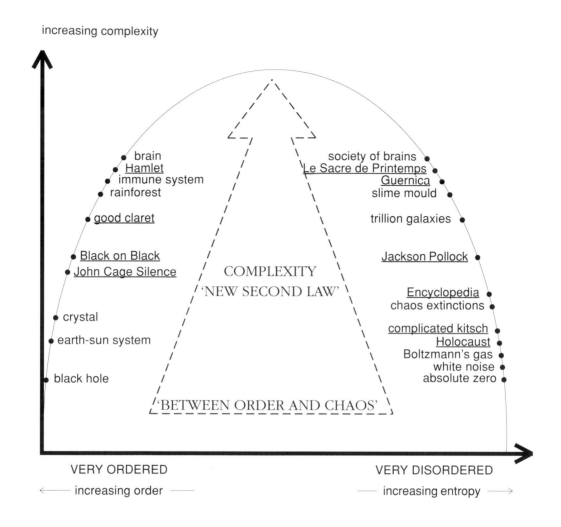

increasing complexity

brain
Hamlet
immune system
rainforest

good claret

Black on Black
John Cage Silence

crystal

earth-sun system

black hole

COMPLEXITY
'NEW SECOND LAW'

'BETWEEN ORDER AND CHAOS'

society of brains
Le Sacre de Printemps
Guernica
slime mould

trillion galaxies

Jackson Pollock

Encyclopedia
chaos extinctions

complicated kitsch
Holocaust
Boltzmann's gas
white noise
absolute zero

VERY ORDERED

← increasing order ——

VERY DISORDERED

—— increasing entropy →

Cosmic Axiology – a formal measure of simplicity, complexity and complication
Illustrated here is one value system that relates to the fundamental processes of the universe. Very simple systems which are ordered are to the left, very complicated systems to the right, and on the 'edge between order and chaos' are systems which extract higher levels of organization from both order and chaos. The argument of this book is that higher organizational states, and the direction of evolution, are 'better' than both very ordered and chaotic systems. If my argument is right then the 'New Second Law', for which 'Complexitists' search, would be one *cosmic system of value, although hardly the only one. In this diagram cultural and natural systems are put on one scale, an obvious simplification as is the notional weighting of each system. Furthermore, the context for cultural measurement is not supplied and thus the ordering is merely formal. Even with these oversimplifications the diagram does reveal a basic structure of formal value. The implications of this diagram are discussed in the next two chapters and that on 'the Edge of Chaos'.*

lar language of description, and culture of those doing it, have to be taken into account – which is theoretically possible, but not done here. In this sense my diagram of value is showing only the formal simplicity and complexity of a work of art, and not its cultural context. There is, of course, more to evaluating a work than gauging its organizational depth, but this is one of the basic axes of value.

Perhaps the 'Complexitists' should come out of the closet and simply pronounce complexity better than simplicity – rather as Herbert Spencer did a hundred years ago. When it does not regress, evolution proceeds from the simple to the complex. The history of the universe has this direction, and we can assume progress equals further complexity (until things get too complicated and, like an overloaded bureaucracy or an overly-complex jet liner such as Concord, communication between the parts becomes strained).

The rainforest is one of the most robust ecosystems (as long as one does not chop it down), and a 'climax' ecosystem is thought to be stronger than a 'pioneer' growth. In both cases a complex web of organisms has redundancy and variety built into it. This multivalence can cope with challenges, diseases and threats more robustly than a simple, new growth. Likewise, a highly developed civilization is regarded as stronger and, yes, even 'better' than a 'primitive' one (dubious proposition though that is). The general trend towards complexity in nature and culture is often assumed to bring with it higher and higher levels of sensitivity, feeling, discrimination, subtlety, holism, creativity – all things that we recognize as 'higher', 'progressive', in short, 'good'.

By contrast the reverse of complexity is not just simplicity but also entropy. The more highly organized a structure is, such as the brain, the more it resists entropy. Growing life and complexity have always been intuitively understood as countering the basic Second Law of Thermodynamics, which holds that a closed system must always run down, become more disorganized, suffer dissipation and finally die. In fact the primary search of Complexitists is for 'the New Second Law', which will explain the spontaneous growth of the universe towards higher levels of what is ridiculously called negentropy, negative entropy. Modern nihilism has such a stranglehold that we phrase the most positive thing in the universe – creative growth – by a double negative!

My diagram (opposite), represents complexity on axes that bring out its relationships with simplicity *and* entropy. In this cosmic axiology (or natural system of value), entropy, the necessary unravelling of time, can be considered 'bad', 'evil', 'sinful' in the sense that most theologies condemn destruction, boredom, dissolution, decline, killing and kitsch (cultural entropy).

To analyze the diagram further, on the bottom axis, to the left, are those very simple deterministic systems that repeat themselves again and again: the earth-sun system that Newton used as his prime example of nature, or the black on black canvasses (produced by Modern artists in the 1910s and *again* in the 1950s). Both natural and cultural systems can be described by relatively short algorithms, or rules for generating these things. To the far right are those entropic systems, very chaotic things which burn up endless computer time in description: for instance, second-rate copies of a Jackson Pollock, all the people in the New York telephone directory, or 'white noise' (the hubbub at a very large cocktail party in a very small room).

Between these two extremes, and at right angles to them, are those things which have higher and higher levels of organization: the immune system, a rainforest, and the most complex things we know in the universe – the human brain and a society of brains. Great works of art are analogues of this cosmic organization, this virtue of the universe: *Hamlet*, a dense well-functioning urban village, *Guernica*, Master chess, *The Name of the Rose*, a fourteen-course *Kaiseki* dinner, *Le Sacre de Printemps*, an extra-innings baseball game, Le Corbusier's *Ronchamp*. I cut across disciplines to emphasize that the quality of organization is at stake in all cases. What is the difference between a good and bad wine; what distinctions are sought in those pretentiously mixed metaphors that attempt to capture the depth and integrity of an old Claret?

We spontaneously value wine, music, architecture and much art with metaphors which point to the complexity and depth of organization.

A Post-Modern ethics, a Post-Christian morality, might come to terms with this fact and generalize a cosmic axiology that includes both natural and cultural systems. The implications can be seen pulled together in the diagram, where the highest degree of organization is represented as a hill to climb, located between order and chaos. Artists climb it as they progress in mastering their work, species climb it as they evolve, the brain climbs it as it understands more and more. As we will see, this place between the two extremes is emphasized by Complexitists as the area of maximum creativity in the universe (see Chapter XV 'Edge of Chaos and Purpose in the Universe').

We can also find in the diagram the two basic arrows of time: the Second Law of Thermodynamics which winds everything down and, at right angles to it, the 'New Second Law', awaiting exact formulation, which is the purposeful direction of cosmic evolution. In the end such an axiology might dramatize what amounts to a cosmic battle between evil and good: the forces of entropy (mass extinctions, asteroids hitting the earth, the Holocaust, warfare, negative-sum games) and the forces of increasing complexity (self-organization, organic evolution, creativity in the arts and sciences, and homeorhesis – or homeostasis over time).

VII
THE IDEAL POET

Previous periods have discovered some of the important factors which lead to greater degrees of organization. For instance the Romantics, especially Samuel Taylor Coleridge, emphasized the difference in quality between works of the imagination and labors of the fancy. The binding and transformative power of the imagination works, as he said, when in the poet's mind there is 'a more than usual state of emotion, with more than usual order'.

According to a basic law of Complexity science, 'more is different': things pushed far-from-equilibrium suddenly organize at a higher level. The poem is pushed up the organizational hill when the creative powers are 'more than usual'. In other words, it works in excess, when both passion and reason are simultaneously combined and tuned up.[10] Great works of art are not produced through moderation, but by the combination of excessive and different states of the personality. Coleridge rightly uses a chemical metaphor for the transformative power of the imagination, and he emphasizes that it unites multiple faculties – much more than just passion and reason – 'the whole soul':

> The poet, described in ideal perfection, brings the whole soul of man into activity, with the subordination of its faculties to each other, according to their relative worth and dignity. He diffuses a tone and spirit of unity, that blends, and (as it were) fuses, each into each, by that synthetic and magical power to which we have exclusively appropriated the name of Imagination.[11]

Today we would no longer speak of pure 'faculties of the whole soul' that have a set 'worth and dignity', but we would acknowledge that a real creative act does fuse opposites and brings unity to disparate material. He continues, setting the synergetic power of imagination against the additive work of fancy:

> This [Imaginative] power, first put in action by the will and understanding, and retained under their irremisive though gentle and unnoticed control (*laxis effertur habenis*) reveals itself in the balance or reconciliation of opposite or discordant qualities: of sameness with difference; the individual with the representative; the sense of novelty and freshness with old and familiar objects; a more than usual state of emotion, with more than usual order; judgement ever awake and steady self-possession . . . [11]

This passage reveals the essential point that willpower and understanding do control imagination, but only gently. If they worked too hard, they would produce things of the fancy; that is, a mere combination of 'fixities and definites', an assemblage of dead objects:

> [the IMAGINATION] dissolves, diffuses, dissipates, in order to recreate; or where this process is rendered impossible, yet still at all events it struggles to idealize and unify. It is essentially vital, even as all objects (as objects) are essentially fixed and dead.
> FANCY, on the contrary, has no other counters to play with, but fixities and definites . . . Equally with the ordinary memory the Fancy must receive all its materials ready made from the law of association.[11]

Making allowances for the early nineteenth-century psychology on which they are based, these passages are relevant today. The imagination and fancy (minus their capital I and F) really do describe different processes. The former creatively brings together previously separate material, the latter merely presents an aggregate of diverse things. One is vital and transformative; the other leaves things unchanged.

This distinction is fundamental for judging the quality of art. Allowing the imagination control of 'the whole soul and all its faculties' produces new works of art rich in multiple levels of meaning. This multivalence, or organizational depth, is a direct result of the multiple ways a work has been encoded: through all the senses, with all the faculties, with all the discourses the artist can master.

Put simply, the 'whole soul' produces complexity. Simple art, by contrast, and much Minimal or Complicated Art, is produced by one or a few faculties – intelligence, wit, passion – acting separately.

Complexity Theory also illuminates another aspect of creative quality. Coleridge's high point of creativity, the charged balance of passion and reason, or the mix of 'a more than usual state of emotion, with more than usual order', is in effect what Complexitists call being 'on the edge between order and chaos'. This boundary condition, more simply put 'the edge of chaos', is now understood to be the place of maximum complexity and computability, the only place where life and mind can emerge.[12]

This boundary condition is also another significant parallel between the creative artist and creative nature: it deepens the notion of a cosmic axiology of value by showing that nature and culture both share a fundamental trait. How big is this seemingly thin area? When it is a phase transition between water and ice, it seems to be only a point. One theorist says that although it is very thin, it is also very wide, like the surface of the ocean, the boundary of waves and foam between sky and sea. I have represented it as a broad area on page 36, because so much of importance occurs here; but these creations are relative rarities, and most things in the universe are either too simple or too complicated to occupy the interesting boundary. Nevertheless, as Complexitists contend, everything in nature and culture is pushed toward this creative edge by evolutionary pressures, by natural selection and internal dynamics.

How far-reaching is this natural system of value? It does not appear to illuminate such things as negative experience – pain, misery and suffering. If these are the equivalent, on a psychological level, of entropy, of deterioration, then why do Christians say pain is a good teacher? Neurologists have recently discovered that we learn through pain, and that a particularly painful experience is more deeply etched on our nervous system than one not felt. Furthermore, we learn through negative instances, through refutation: 'experience', as Oscar Wilde said, 'is the name we give to our mistakes'. These examples suggest that we can turn entropy to creative use, as long as it is contained by a will to order. There are many instances of an artist using chance, nonsense, chaos, degradation – sheer idiocy – as a spur to invention and communication. The Surrealist compositional method of 'exquisite corpse', Ionescu's play *The Rhinoceros*, and Frank Gehry's fish buildings are twentieth-century examples which turn the absurd *non sequitur* into a creative art form. Such work forces us to reconsider any fundamentalist notion that entropy, kitsch, pain, or complication are 'bad' in themselves. Rather, when they are isolated on their own, they are negative.

At the other end of the scale, we should distinguish between order and organization, simple regularity and the *density* with which things are linked. Again it is a matter of quality, or multivalence, or organizational depth – all three of which go beyond the customary opposition between complexity and simplicity. So much of the public discussion contrasts order with chaos and then falsely concludes that order *per se* is good. This idea has been dominant since the ancient Egyptians, and since the Christian Bible proclaimed that God created order out of chaos. It might have been more appropriate to have said that organization emerged at the boundary between order and chaos; but it did take two thousand years to discover this.

Lastly, this axiology refers to the way creativity is carried out, the inventiveness and depth of the language, *not* the content expressed. As I have mentioned in discussing Peter Fuller, it is natural to confuse creativity, language and value, because they are always experienced together, but they have to be analytically separated if we are going to have a more cosmological architecture. It is the language and content to which we now turn.

PART TWO

IN WHICH LANGUAGE SHALL WE BUILD?

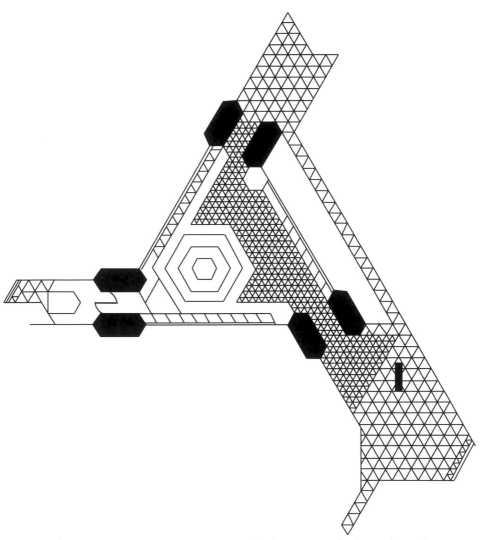

Bruce Goff, Joe Price Studio, Bartlesville, Oklahoma, 1956, plan. *The self-similarity which all fractals show is not self-sameness. Here triangles, hexagons, tribexes, lozenges and other shapes transform the same angles at all scales and in different materials.*

VIII

SELF-SIMILARITY (FRACTALS) AND STRANGE ATTRACTORS

We have seen the inadequacy of Modern architecture, and the necessity for creating an architecture of organizational depth, but that still leaves important questions open. Is there one language of architecture which is more suited to the contemporary situation than another? Is there an answer to the perennial question – asked since the early nineteenth century – 'in which style shall we build?' Before taking on this recurrent query I will examine several of the emergent languages which are inspired by, or revealing of, Complexity and Chaos theories. In these chapters I will touch on nine or so identifiable departures of the last several years, starting with the analogies which have become so familiar with the emrgence of Chaos Theory.

Fractals, the fractional dimensions lying between the customary one-, two- and three-dimensions, can be found throughout all of nature. They measure the crinkliness of things, like a wad of paper squeezed together, or the coastline of Scotland, which is so complex in its doubling back that it approaches three-dimensions. Clouds, coastlines, snowflakes, ferns and trees are fractals showing an important quality that Benoit Mandelbrot pointed out: self-similarity. In a typical fractal object, parts resemble not only other parts, but the whole. This self-similarity is a transformational similitude – not an exact replication – a point that has been stressed in poetics since Aristotle.

Self-similarity is positive whereas self-sameness, monotony – the monothematatis of Modernism – is boring. So is complete dissimilarity, chaos.

Virtually all those who referred to 'organic architecture' (including classicists, such as Vitruvius and Alberti, and Modernists, such as Gropius and Wright) insisted on work that shows self-similarity. 'Unity *with* variety'. 'Organic unity, where not a part can be added or subtracted except for the worse' are injunctions that have rebounded through the halls of building sites for 2,000 years.

It is a truism that all organisms and architecture must show some self-similarity and the influence of strange attractors, but architecture that is rich in both – the Gothic, the Beaux Arts – is contrasted, by Benoit Mandelbrot, with the curtain-walled lifelessness of Modern architecture. Modern architecture, the International Style, and the Machine Aesthetic, usually have no focus, no climax about the entrance, middle or top (typical attractors); nor do they usually vary a single motif at all, let alone in a thousand ways (self-similarity).

By contrast, those who style themselves 'organic architects' often mimic nature's patterns of organization and, in designs, 'naturally' repeat a formal idea at many scales and, just as inevitably as a flower, provide several focii. Bruce Goff is exemplary in this respect. Self-similar triangles, hexagons and trihexes organize his Price House – from the very large to the very smallest detail. Sixty degree angles, their multiplication and subdivision, recur in all sorts of forms and materials. While Goff designed well before the science of fractals was conceived, like his mentor Frank Lloyd Wright he virtually invented fractalian architecture before the fact. All his buildings obsessively transform geometric forms, and the Price House is typical in this respect. Its conversation 'pit' is hexagonal, the walls of the music room are triangular to deflect sound, and various self-similar wedge-shapes emerge from the ceiling in the form of acoustic decoration. These are constructed from – I have not made this up – 'plastic rain', green string and goose feathers, which act also to soften the crystalline forms.

With the Bavinger and Garvey Houses (1950 and 1952 respectively), Goff uses a strange attractor to organize a force-field of movement around and up a ramp. A strange attractor, like the Red Spot of Jupiter or turbulence in the flow of water, is the chaotic but still ordered organization of movement around maxima and minima. Picture it as a fluctuating electron cloud zipping around the core of the nucleus: never in the same place exactly, but always attracted within one orbit or another. Or imagine it as the turbulent eddies that collect behind rocks in a fast-moving stream: they jump around chaotically but are attracted to the same general area. In Goff's Bavinger House one stops at various room 'pods' – point attractors – which curve off the overall route, and it is this which acts as a strange attractor. The spiral route both attracts motion and visual direction, but it does so differently at each ascent and descent, thus approaching that mixture of deterministic chaos so familiar since Edward Lorenz pointed it out.

  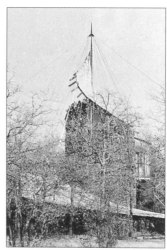

LEFT and CENTER: Bruce Goff, Price House, *interior and exterior, 1956-76. Fractal shapes extend through the glass cullet, details and structure; RIGHT: Bruce Goff,* Bavinger House, *Norman, Oklahoma, 1950. A fifty-foot mast holds the roof and underscores the strange attractors of the spiral shapes as they oscillate through the rubble masonry.*

Particularly important at the Bavinger House is the way Goff absorbs industrial and natural ready-mades into his fractal language, producing the most heterogeneous of architectural languages: thrown-away rocks and glass cullet, discarded walnut trees, stainless steel cables (biplane braces which were being thrown out), a mast from an oil rig that was no longer needed, fishnet for balconies and, the ultimate ad hocery, a former bomber's blister used for a lighting fixture. That his fractal language could absorb such heterogeneous material from nature *and* culture is a lesson to all practicing architects, even that great *bricoleur* Frank Gehry.

In spite of the pun, I am tempted to call Goff a 'natural' cosmic architect: his theory and training did not lead him here, his explanations of his work did not, of course, refer to strange attractors, but he unconsciously derived such organizational forms by consciously following nature's grammar and processes. Recycle everything, organize a building like a flowing stream, a self-similar cloud or cracked ice, and you may derive such a grounded architecture.

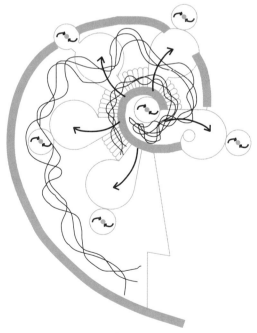

FROM LEFT TO RIGHT: Bruce Goff, Bavinger House, *interior, 'bomber blister' as point attractor below fish-net pod;* Bavinger plan *shows strange attractor of spiral movement. In the center it oscillates chaotically around the stairway and on the edges within limit cycles of walls. Five larger and six smaller point-attractors are suspended pods.*

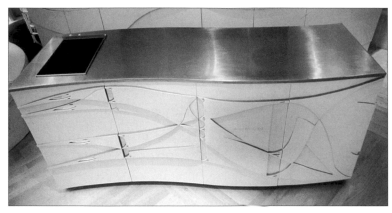

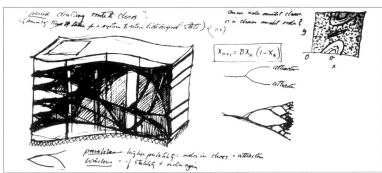

Charles Jencks, Organization Emerging in Chaos, *Scotland, 1992. The Rabbit Cabinet, an overall s-curve, shows in its ornament the period-doubling route to increasing chaos. The undulating graph, generated by the feedback equation $X_{n+1} = BX_n (1-X_n)$ has the typical set of bifurcation points which settle around attractors. As the mother rabbit has more children, the population doubles towards increasing chaos, but then – amazingly – jumps back into self-similar order three times (indicated by the vertical voids). Parabolic curves reveal further organization hidden in the randomness. The rest of the room also shows nonlinear behaviour.*

IX

NONLINEARITY

We all are well acquainted with the concept of feedback – the way a micro-phone can amplify noise back on itself until it screams, or the way populations of rabbits can experience runaway growth, then collapse to a much reduced number. Such examples of nonlinear change are quite different from the results of linear mechanics – or straight-line determinism – that underlay the Newtonian world-view. The Modern world saw the universe as developing regularly along a line that the physicist and mathematician could plot. It was the goal of Modern science to explain all phenomena as essentially variants of this orderly behav-iour. In the last twenty years, however, a reverse hypothesis has grown, which supposes that most of the universe is nonlinear (whatever 'most' means). If the supposition is right, then architecture ought to reflect it.

In the same twenty years a different kind of equation has come to the fore: the nonlinear variety, which relays back information into itself. These second-order equations characteristically have terms which compete with each other, such as those in the Verhulst equation which deals with population dynamics:

$$X_{n+1} = BX_n(1-X_n).$$

Here the two competing terms are X_n and $(1-X_n)$ because, as the first one grows, the second one diminishes. The equation is quite predictive of the way populations will double their size until they go into deterministic chaos, a chaos that shows some emergent order. This combination of order and chaos is fantas-tic, paradoxical, counter-intuitive. One can well imagine that, if rabbits keep multiplying, the total numbers might fluctuate as they climb upwards (or until owls and ferrets get to work). But why should the numbers suddenly return to a very simple order, and just a few rabbits?

It is because of the maths. It sounds implausible, especially if you have too many rabbits in the garden. Nevertheless, the maths entail this fascinating order amid chaos. If one wants to figure the equation out, X_n represents last year's population, B represents the birth rate of the rabbits, and X_{n+1} represents the prediction for this year's population based on last year.

Rather than belabouring the reader with the precise unravelling of this equa-tion, I illustrate it with a piece of furniture I have designed for a place in Scot-land, where the rabbit population fluctuates somewhat in accordance with the maths. Starting from the left of the storage cabinet, one can see the four basic strange attractors pulling the total population size to one of four places. Then as one reads to the right, and as the female rabbits have more offspring, these attractors bifurcate to eight attractors, then sixteen, and so forth until the mother gives birth to approximately 3.6 on average. At this point the total population could be anywhere within the parabolic swirls; the system has gone into deterministic chaos. And yet it still has some order. This is indicated by the depth of the parabolic swirls, their continuation across the whole surface and, most surprisingly, the way that, at three points, the three vertical lines, the system returns suddenly to its original bifurcations!

Then the previous simple order re-emerges for a very short period, just before it bursts into deeper chaos. But even there, when the populations could be nearly anywhere – illustrated far right of the cabinet – there is still *some* predictability, some likelihood that will favour certain numbers over others. These probabilities are, again, shown by the thicker parabolas. The parabolas and bifurcations swirl through the whole surface, so the ornament has that canonic 'unity in variety' that is so prevalent in nature. Similar parabolic themes of growth and sudden change are taken up elsewhere in the room, but always transformed.

Why highlight such growth (called period-doubling) and nonlinearity? One reason is that most Complexitists, such as Joseph Ford, believe that most of nature is nonlinear:

> . . . non-chaotic systems are very nearly as scarce as hen's teeth, despite the fact that our physical understanding of nature is largely based upon their study.[13]

This truth, which is beginning to be accepted, is quite incredible. For most of history we have focused on the tiny fraction of things that showed a simple order – perhaps because of a profound desire to control nature – and then assumed the rest was like this. But while mechanistic things, like the two-body experiment of the sun and earth's rotation, and ballistics, can be explained by linear equations, the rest of nature cannot. Yet, as I have asked, what does this 'most', or 'rest' mean? Ninety-five per cent? It appears to Complexitists that it constitutes all that is living, chemical, unfolding and thermodynamic – thus, even galaxies. Or perhaps more than ninety-nine per cent of nature?

Whatever the case, I have tried to represent nonlinearity, period doubling and feedback through an architecture of waves and twists, an architecture that undulates and grows and diminishes continuously *and* abruptly. The smooth growth of a wave form represents the continuity of nature, its unity and harmony, whereas the sudden twist represents the catastrophes of nature, the flip from one system to another, or the creative bifurcations which can bring progress as well as despair. Since nature shows these two properties might not a cosmogenic architecture represent these two basic truths?

X
AN ARCHITECTURE OF WAVES AND TWISTS

Why give so much emphasis to an architecture of undulating forms? The partial answer is that wave motion, like nonlinearity, is so crucial and omnipresent in nature. At a basic level, in the microworld of quantum physics, the wave function of the atom is as fundamental as the particulate aspect. Every subatomic particle is both wave and particle. Every object and human being is composed of this bipolar unity, this double entity. The wave aspect is masked to us, however, because it is unobservable compared to our relatively huge size.

Some physicists believe, moreover, that thought is basically a wave phenomenon. This is intuitively obvious; after all, an idea weighs nothing, is contained all over the brain, is stretched out like a wave, can travel near the speed of light, and is changeable like an ocean wave. Quantum waves also have, like thoughts, paradoxical properties: unlike particles and objects, they can tunnel through walls – a miracle that happens in every television set. A wave form is also the superposition of many small waves and thus, like a thought, can contain many contradictory states within itself without collapsing. It is a truism of psychology today to say that the self is constructed of many contradictory parts (child self, parent self, worker self, leisure self, and so on) just as it is a truism to say we often have many contradictory thoughts struggling in our mind at once – voices superimposed on each other and held in suspension, just as a quantum wave is the superposition of many smaller waves.

Quantum waves can add up, cancel, go through each other, and be in several places at once. In short, the wave form contains the properties well known as 'quantum weirdness', the paradoxical and essential mind-quality of the universe.[14] This is not the place to discuss the extraordinary aspects of quantum mechanics, but the wave form and function are so basic and important in the universe that it *is* the place to emphasize the fundamental place they should have in architecture.

I have been particularly drawn to representing the strange phenomenon of the soliton wave, because it shows the coherence of a nonlinear feedback system, and something approaching 'memory'. The Red Spot of Jupiter is a soliton, as are the tidal bores that can reach twenty-five feet in height and travel at a constant speed for five hundred miles. Solitons were first theorized by the Scottish engineer John Scott Russell in 1834, after he had an unusual experience while riding his horse along the Union Canal near Edinburgh:

> I was observing the motion of a boat which was rapidly drawn along a narrow channel by a pair of horses when the boat suddenly stopped –

not so the mass of water in the channel which it had put in motion; it accumulated round the prow of the vessel in a state of violent agitation, then suddenly leaving it behind, rolled forward with great velocity, assuming the form of a large solitary elevation, a rounded, smooth and well defined heap of water, which continued its course along the channel apparently without change of form or diminution of speed. I followed it on horseback, and overtook it still rolling on at a rate of some eight or nine miles an hour, preserving its original figure some thirty feet long and a foot to a foot-and-a-half in height. Its height gradually diminished, and after a chase of one or two miles I lost it in the windings of the channel.[15]

Russell's solitary wave, or soliton, keeps its identity instead of dissipating, as do normal waves because the smaller waves that constitute it bounce back and reinforce the overall shape and frequency. This feedback is the reverse of turbulence. It is obviously balanced on the delicate edge between order and chaos: if the width or depth of the canal is varied greatly, the resonance will not occur. Given the coherence of such waves, they can do unusual things, such as pass intact through each other. Or a high, thin, humpbacked soliton can overtake a short, fat one, combine for a while as a single wave, and then re-emerge, as if the two remembered their separate identities. Solitons have been found in such diverse systems as planetary atmospheres, crystals, plasmas, and nerve fibres, and have been created for such systems as superconductors and optical fibres.

In general they can be considered as focused energy waves, or coherent patterns. They can be represented in two basic ways: either as the travelling *hump* in a whiplash or as the *twist* in a flat strip, such as a leather belt. The second is 'topologically trapped' and can be eliminated only by an anti-twist. 'Humps' and 'twists' are two signs I have used, especially in a series of metal gates to represent the travelling of focused energy through the universe.

These show waves of energy moving from the points of focus, or structure – here the latch or hinges. They travel across the gate diagonally, giving a kind of visual energy that is accentuated by the alternation of solid and void, black and white, foreground and background. The twists appear almost absent, so the represented soliton seems to pass through the gate to the points that hold it, and where it opens. The latch is further focused by a twisted Mobius Strip, itself an endless form, and a spiral fossil, which also takes up the curvilinear geometry. Sometimes the soliton even travels, at least visually, into the stone wall. Thus natural and designed wave forms are merged.

I find depicting solitons compelling, not only because of their aesthetic energy but also because of their inspiration in a new science. They represent deeper aspects of the natural world that are just being discovered, and I believe architecture should always engage with such investigation. Even if it should not situate itself exclusively at the edge of knowledge, architecture needs always to be pushing the frontiers – not just of technology and materials, but of science and our understanding of ourselves. I believe we are most fascinated by this art when it is conveying something in a beautiful language that we did not know before. Perhaps this is because, of all definitions applied to us, we are 'the learning animal'. Our aesthetic enjoyment and pleasure in life are deeply tied to curiosity, adaptation, the will to discover new truths; and this drive has to be put at the center of a new philosophy.

Plato, Nietzsche and Freud were wrong – it is not immortality, power and sex which drives us (important as they may be) – but *learning*. The whole universe is trying to discover its own being, and we are at the forefront of this cosmic lust for knowledge, as I will argue further in the last section.

Charles Jencks, Soliton Gates, *Scotland, 1993. Twists of waves travel towards center and edge, latch and support, punctuated by fossils.*

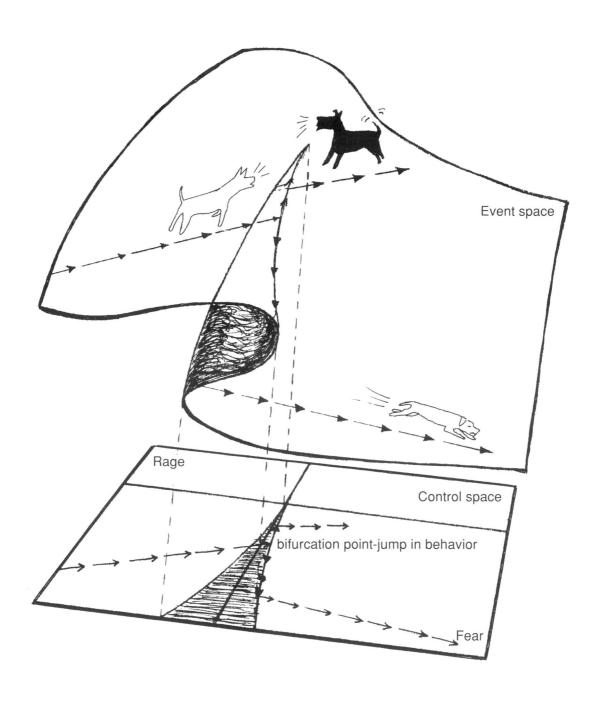

Event space

Rage

Control space

bifurcation point-jump in behavior

Fear

Cusp-Catastrophe. *The indigenous dog, to the left, follows a linear behaviour on a 'map' of two control variables – fear and rage – until it reaches the fold (edge of chaos) at which point a slight change in the dog's mood, or situation, has a catastrophic effect on behaviour– which now jumps either way, to flight or fight. The catastrophe-fold can represent all sorts of situations from prison riots, and decision-making to sea-waves. (After John Briggs, F David Peat and René Thom).*

XI
FOLDING – CATASTROPHE AND CONTINUITY

Another related wave form, the fold, has also emerged from recent science and the Catastrophe Theory of René Thom. Catastrophe Theory is not primarily concerned with what we call catastrophes but, rather, the more prosaic 'phase transitions' that are everywhere visible in nature: the dramatic transformation of water into ice at zero degrees centigrade, or into steam at one hundred degrees centigrade; the sudden transformation of a corn kernel into popcorn; the sudden emergence of a rainbow. Phase transitions occur when systems are pushed far from equilibrium by adding heat, energy or information. They can be represented in two different ways: either by a bifurcation of one linear development into two lines or by a fold, twist, pleat, or crushed plane.

In architecture the cracked ice pattern in Chinese trellis is one sign of 'catastrophe'. In the West the ruined castle, or eighteenth-century ruin, or broken column are others.

René Thom has identified seven elementary types of catastrophe. The first two are represented by folds. The second type (which interests me) is the 'cusp catastrophe', which can be pictured as a gently folded sheet of paper. This sheet represents two dimensions of control (two variables or forces) because it has two axes. A well-known illustration of this type involves an animal motivated by conflicting emotions, fear and rage. A dog on its own territory is approached by another dog and starts barking madly to scare it off. As the intruder approaches, also growling, it reveals itself as bigger and stronger. Yet, since the indigenous dog is inspired by a sense of ownership, it does not run away but engages in further furious warnings.

If you map the dog's increasing rage across a sheet of paper, it rises towards the fold – a straight line of escalating symbolic warfare. It then reaches a point of uncertainty and travels along it – the fold – which is at a different angle from the approach. Fight or flight? Give into rage or fear? This edge between order and chaos is travelled for a short time and then – catastrophe – the indigenous dog runs off. That generates yet another line, in a different direction. This same sequence of behaviour (fight-uncertainty-catastrophe-flight) can be represented either as a bifurcation sequence or a fold.

The fold as a technique in architecture can accomplish opposite qualities: it can represent a sudden change of direction, assumption, or mood – the dog's jump from fight to flight. Conversely it can resolve differences in a way which is distinct from the other architectural methods of dealing with pluralism, such as collage. This is by *enfolding*, by connecting that which is different in a smooth transition. Here suppleness and smoothness are important – the way, for instance, that two different liquids are enfolded into each other by stirring.

I have used the fold in both ways: in furniture to show the twisting play of structural forces and the tensile forces of fabric. The fold literally bends the fabric in a fan-shape to be able to move over a curved surface and still be pulled to a corner – opposite roles which the fold resolves. In landscape, it is used to orient movement first towards a central lake and then towards a field, resolving the opposite views in a smooth continuity. In ornament I have used it to turn undulating lines into a functional handle – a clear use of the enfolding, reconciling aspect – while in a detail I have used it to show the abrupt move from one

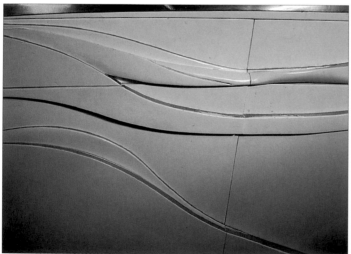

Charles Jencks, Scotland, 1993. FROM ABOVE, LEFT TO RIGHT: Fabric folds of a Twist Couch *are pulled in tension to structural points enfolding a complex curve;* Snakes *in the landscape orient in opposite directions as paths fold over;* Handles *emerge as folds from the ornament; an* Overhead Twist *is warped to connect two different axes.*

system to another. This last is closest to the cusp catastrophe of René Thom, because it signals a sudden shift in the frame of reference, the bifurcation point. The fold dramatizes change and contradiction – the quick transition from one system of meaning to another – without trying to resolve them.

An architect who has taken this to the extreme of an entire building and neighborhood plan is Peter Eisenman. Several of his folded buildings in Japan look as if the underground tectonic plates pushed against each other, creating earthquakes, and have erupted into the structure, making it collapse. Indeed, his intention is, in part, to represent this omnipresent form of catastrophe, especially because it is so much on the mind of the Japanese. The results are interesting, amusing, sometimes beautiful and even appropriate – although in the end they may seem wilful and annoying in an office building, since one does not want to be reminded of the Big One every day.

More subtle are his folded designs for Rebstock Park on the outskirts of Frankfurt. Here we find a more gentle folding process, in which the perimeter block of traditional housing is combined with the linear *siedlung* of Modernist practice. The Post-Modern hybrid of old and 1920s urbanism is convincing because they are enfolded into each other. The two types are interwoven by rhythmical waves that wash across the site. It is true that the process introduces dislocations and awkward collisions, which no doubt Eisenman sought; but these are also bent into the details, giving the whole a self-similarity, a unity of part and whole.

I am reminded here of the physicist David Bohm and his emphasis on the way the universe *enfolds* an 'implicate order' (the ultimate, connected reality behind things) and *unfolds* the explicate order that we see – a continuous double process. Enfolding is the unifying force of the universe, unfolding is the evolutionary force of the pluriverse. Although Eisenman does not base his work on Bohm's model, it looks as if he did.[16] We can see the presence of the linear Modern blocks (especially appropriate because many were built in Frankfurt in the 1920s) and the traditional perimeter blocks, as well as the combination of both. It is the inbetween area, however, that dominates. The fold, the ambiguous area of catastrophe that connects both frames of reference, is omnipresent.

In a similar manner Zaha Hadid has used the fold to reconcile building, landscape and urban space. Characteristically she warps a rectangular model, pushes here, pulls there and stretches it as if it were rubber. This gives what she calls 'planetary architecture' supple elasticity. Her buildings seem to leave the ground from which they cantilever as long, stretched, angular space-ships. Her cosmic gestures are usually painted against an absolute black of outer space, white spectres leaving their streamlined trails as they pass through the heavens.

Although firmly attached to the ground and static, her architecture of movement is a natural sign of cosmogenesis. Like the Futurists, her concrete monu-

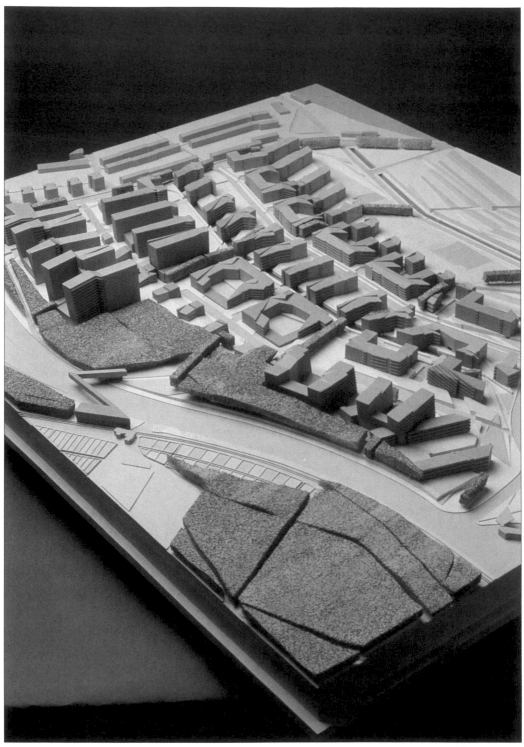

ABOVE and OPPOSITE, LEFT: Peter Eisenman, Rebstock Park Housing, *Frankfurt, 1992. Organizational waves move through the site and merge landscape and two types of housing – Modern slab and traditional perimeter block. This hybridization is a subtle, creative and beautiful version of Post-Modern double-coding taken into the elevations and details.*

ments are symbolic of change, dynamism and cutting through space – not actually performative.

Hadid's recent winning design for the Cardiff Bay Opera House in Wales is a case in point. Here the service elements wrap around the interior auditorium, as she says, like the jewels of a necklace turned inside-out. The basic rectangular block holds the street-lines and creates an internal semi-public piazza which is then – like the Piazza San Marco in Venice – opened out at one point towards the sea. This opening stretches the whole building into the prow of a ship – the rubber rectangle is distorted in the direction of primary orientation. Thus people will naturally flock back and forth between a semi-protected and completely open landscape. Hadid further enfolds such spatial movement into the section and plan of the auditorium which is another basic polygon stretched towards the sea. In effect, the fold is used here not just literally to fold over wall, ceiling and floor planes, but also as a connective device to create unity. Difference is enfolded into a continuity.

Several other architects – Greg Lynn, Jeffrey Kipnis, and Bahram Shirdel – have investigated the fold as a compositional method, and an issue of *Architectural Design* is devoted to the subject.[17] While it would be premature to judge the results of a recent architectural movement, one can say it already shows affinities with the crystalline architecture of the Czech Cubists, a point to which I will return in conclusion. One exciting aspect of this architecture is that it returns us to the ambiguity of the natural, growing world of crystals in which plan, section and elevation are reconfigured in an ambiguous way. Much of nature is like this, just as scientists are insisting that 'most' of nature is nonlinear.

The question, again, resides in the meaning of 'most'. Is nature mostly crystalline, or undulating, or catastrophic? It depends on the time-scale and the subject of investigation. When we look at long periods of evolution they show less punctuations than equilibria, fewer periods of sudden creativity than slow, gradual change. Consider earthquakes in the city where I sometimes live, Los Angeles.

RIGHT: Peter Eisenman, Nunotani Headquarters, *Tokyo 1992. The building records compressions, earthquake pressures and a phallocentric skyscraper suddenly 'limp'.*

Most of the time the large tectonic plates are moving too slowly to register jolts on the Richter scale. When there is a big earthquake – every hundred and twenty years or so – it is an historical event. Subsequent earthquakes which always follow it, aftershocks, occur in the proportion of many tiny ones, few medium size ones, and very few large ones. If we think of the earth as always moving and grinding its plates – which it is – but a major quake as a catastrophe which changes other life, then we see how to consider the frequency of catastrophe. It is a predictable rarity. The major mass-extinctions caused by meteor showers follow the same distribution as the earthquakes. Every day we are bombarded by thousands of these 'shooting stars'; every August we have an extra shower of 'Perseids'; and, according to one theory, every twenty-six million years or so there is a real cosmic catastrophe that hits the earth, and wipes out a considerable number of species.

Which is the most 'real' of these situations, the one which is most normal or rare? Which might we represent in architecture? When we turn to living nature we find a different proportion of catastrophic event to gradual change. Much of the natural world we see around us is, most of the time, in dynamic equilibrium, or homeostasis, or harmonious balance: otherwise it would not stay alive.

For these metaphysical reasons, and because folds and warps are strong, idiosyncratic forms that cry out for attention, I have placed them, in my own work, more on a secondary than primary level. They exist on the surface more often than in section, in ornament more than in plan, though occasionally they go through the whole design.

The fact that, on a macro-scale or over a long time period, nonlinearity is more preponderant in the universe than linearity has been obscured by the history of science which, as it were, got its priorities backwards. This happened because the simple linear sciences were discovered first, and that led to an inversion in our metaphysics, the wrong proportion between order and nonlinearity. Ian Stewart, the British mathematician who has written *Does God Play Dice: the Mathematics of Chaos*, makes this point:

> To call a general differential equation 'nonlinear' is rather like calling zoology 'nonpachydermology'. But you see, we live in a world which for centuries acted as if the only animal in existence was the elephant.[18]

Hence, if one is to represent the metaphysics that Complexity Theory is revealing on the big scale, one arrives at the sublation of linearity within nonlinearity. In architecture, the new metaphysics calls for more continuously changing shapes than repetitive squares – enfolding – set off by the occasional punctuation of a fold.

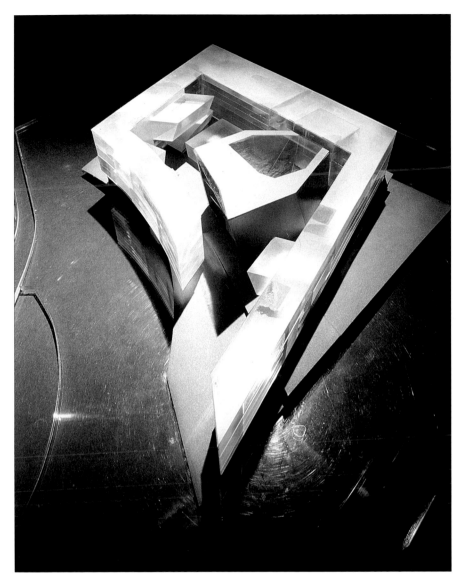

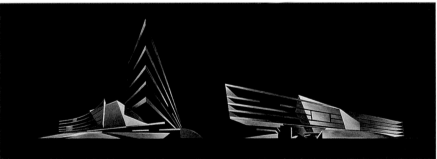

Zaha Hadid, Cardiff Bay Opera House, *competition winner, 1994. A perimeter block en-folds various functions, geometries and central auditorium in a continuous language of planes that are stretched – like distorted rubber – towards the main focus, Cardiff Bay. Anamorphic perspective is combined with oblique folds.*

XII

SUDDEN EMERGENCE – PHASE TRANSITIONS

The sudden, spontaneous emergence of new organizations – unpredicted and underdetermined by the parts – is surely one of the most extraordinary aspects of the universe. Complexity Theory is based on this truth of emergence, even if it cannot fully explain the miraculous power behind it. We are all familiar with sudden phase changes, as I have mentioned, such as the abrupt change from ice to water to vapour, and we are generally familiar with the sudden jumps between one epoch and another – the Gothic to Renaissance, or, for species, the Triassic to Jurassic. Indeed, periods of culture and nature are classified by jumps, as if the universe changed its mind abruptly and decided to go in a new direction. There is also, however, continuity and gradual evolution. And even the more abrupt shifts actually take decades, or even millions of years, although they are sudden on the time-scale of our planet or when placed against the backdrop of the fifteen billion years of the cosmos.

Sudden jumps exist at all scales of nature and are connected to self-organization. Imagine an enzyme that encourages further production of the same enzyme, in runaway growth. This 'auto-catalysis', an example of positive-feedback, may drive the evolution of a species very quickly in a certain direction until it is balanced by 'cross-catalytic' processes, or negative-feedback. Take a completely different field: imagine the global stock market being driven by the idea that economic growth in East Asia was the most robust in the world. These stocks would rise and then, because of the rise, would rise even faster in an 'auto-speculative' fever. The sudden burst in price – doubling the value of these markets as in 1993 – is an upward jump, which was predictably followed, in February 1994, by a sudden descent. This collapse was kicked off by the tiniest rise in American interest rates – half a percent! Because of positive-feedback, self-organizing systems are very sensitive to the smallest signals.

Similar self-organization can be found in 'chemical clocks', which oscillate at regular intervals when energy is added. Ilya Prigogine, a Nobel Prize laureate and physicist, has termed these jumping systems 'dissipative structures' because they dissipate heat as they leap to new levels of self-organization. They have to be continuously pushed 'far from equilibrium', (that is, far from entropy) by the addition of energy, or heat, or information.[19]

Chris Langton, who works at the Santa Fe Institute – which is devoted to Complexity Theory – has produced a helpful diagram which explains the general idea behind emergence, or what I would call 'jumping structures'. It shows local variables interacting together at the bottom, or object-level, and the sudden emergence of a global structure above it, at the meta-level. This holistic entity at the top, the emergent property, then feeds back on the local variables. Examples of this can be found in all living organisms and even superorganisms, such as a beehive, city or any type of social organization.

Take the system of early capitalism as described by Adam Smith in 1776. The free-market mechanism – his 'Society of Perfect Liberty', which miraculously adjusts supply and demand – is also what he called an 'invisible hand'. No one sees it; no one created it; and, like the hand of God, it invisibly manipulates forces. The Hidden Hand turns greed into products a society wants, when and where it wants them, and at an affordable price. Today we may be too well aware of what the free-market does badly, but how does it achieve its benefits? Through the agent of competition. Using Chris Langton's model, we could say that the self-interest of individuals plus a competitive market, at the object-level, creates an emergent structure of capitalism at the meta-level. This emergent global structure, which includes theories such as Adam Smith's, then feeds back on local interactions. The capitalist system shows many such positive feedback loops, including the one that interests the capitalist the most: enormous profit.

Clans, tribes, communities, nations, even nation-states are also emergent structures that come into being spontaneously. Internal forces of organization plus the size of population may push these systems forward. Increasing energy and information – trade, a growing economy – may push them 'far from equilibrium' so that they spontaneously jump from one level to the next, from early capitalism to mercantile capitalism to monopoly capitalism to welfare-state capitalism. Of course political and social theorists understand a little of this, and society passes laws and social programs which strengthen the emergent structure, but largely it emerges unconsciously as a product of interactions at the local level. Both the capitalist system and nation-state then feedback on the local variables that gave them birth – and they literally feed off them, too.

Obviously, all new architecture gives birth to an emergent order that did not previously exist – the social group that may use the building – but only rarely

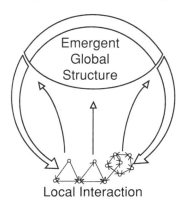

Emergent Global Structure

Local Interaction

Chris Langton, Emergence Diagram, *1992, shows interacting components – pushed far from equilibrium – jumping to global structure which then feeds back on the components. All complex systems exhibit these sudden organizational jumps. The philosopher, C Lloyd Morgan, first developed such ideas in* Emergent Evolution, *1923, according to which 2 + 2 ≠ 4; rather 2 + 2 = apples. In emergence theory, as the Noble laureate Philip Anderson wrote in a key article of 1972, 'More is Different'.*

does it *create* an emergent social order, or building type. Perhaps a recent example is Daniel Libeskind's Jewish Museum addition to the German Museum in Berlin, which creates, from the fact of the Holocaust and the deportation of Jews from Berlin, a new kind of order: that of the dual-national building and the 'wandering' structure. Look at the plan and details: the zig-zags, skewed forms, fractures and jumps in direction. These show many aspects that the Complexity Theory illuminates – self-similarity, nonlinearity, and organizational depth – but above all the abrupt change in direction that is a phase change. Obviously Libeskind did not set out to illustrate this *per se*, nor the theory of sudden emergence. Yet because his characteristic grammar of design has a fractal quality and is based on a metaphysics of cosmic complication – the presentation of opposites – it naturally reveals cataclysmic shifts and violent change.

The 'void' down the non-center of the new museum symbolizes the unthinkable nature of the Holocaust, the unrepresentable fact that 240,000 Berlin Jews were uprooted from their homes and deported to their death. The crime has an architectural consequence; particularly so in this case because for so long Albert Speer, the architect and minister in charge of transforming Nazi Berlin – remember the Spreebogen competition mentioned at the outset of this book – denied knowledge of the resettlement. The void represents this unspeakable truth in a rather unfathomable way: it is a non-place to which one continually returns but on which one cannot walk, a space to go towards but never be in. It acts holistically over the parts, pulling them together just as does the common zinc material and the transformation of fractured forms (the fractals). This strange and haunting museum is a seminal building of the 1990s, and one of the aspects that makes it so is its emergent language and form, two things that keep it from being assimilated into ordinary discourse.

Can one generalize from these few remarks? Phase transitions and sudden emergence characterize all life and history. Indeed the story of history, as we will see, is the narrative of phase transitions; the sudden jumps in nature and culture from one level of organization often to a higher one. There are regres-

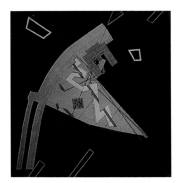 

Daniel Libeskind, Jewish Museum, *extension to Berlin Museum, Berlin, 1989-95.*

sions and setbacks which can be sudden also, but they lie within an overall progressive account. How can this chequered story be represented in architecture – except by sudden surprises, quick changing discontinuities and fractured forms? Perhaps. But as Robert Venturi has long insisted, it would also have to show an 'obligation to the difficult whole', the continuities and unities which are as much an essential of life. The aesthetic of emergence contrasts the difficult whole with the fractured surprise.

The architect, like the ecologist, is somewhat in the role of a god creating new worlds; but a god with an imperfect command of emergence. Some of the recipes, laws and rules of thumb produce well-known consequences, but when a new building or new town springs to life there is always an unpredictable element of self-organization (otherwise it would not be alive).

The philosophical question is whether the architect can predetermine emergence – for that is what the client, in effect, demands. The answer is 'yes and no'. When ecologists experiment with many new micro-climates in order to create the end-state they desire, they find that the order in which they add different species makes a different whole emerge. Sequence and succession, as well as elements, matter. Because of feedback, slight differences in the sequence or the element may create a different emergent. By analogy, the architect knows a lot about the deterministic order that is likely to emerge in a building, and a great deal about the order in which parts should be added to the structure – what else are blueprints and schedules than an attempt to fix succession? Yet any good architect also knows the key to a great building is taking advantage of surprises – both negative and positive. *There must be an unpredictable emergent* in a creative building, or city, and that leads to two consequences. In the end, there is no shorter program or smaller model than the building itself and, secondly, to exploit surprising wholes, the architect must pay close attention to the process.

If fortune favours the prepared mind, then emergence favours those who watch for serendipity. Great architecture exploits accident.

Daniel Libeskind, Jewish Museum, *extension to Berlin Museum, Berlin, 1989-95.*

XIII

ORGANIZATIONAL DEPTH

The obligation towards the whole *and* part, *and* conflict *and* unity, introduces Robert Venturi's other central notion, that of 'contradiction'. This concept was first developed by many architects in the 1970s, when they started to deal with the consequences of cultural pluralism. During that decade it became apparent that there was no one, single society for which the architect could design. While Modernists had appealed to a social abstraction, 'the people' (and many Modernists continue to do so today) it became clear that this concept masked social heterogeneity, different interest groups, ethnic groups, and struggling individuals. Of course 'the people' of a nation *do* exist, *pace* Margaret Thatcher, who famously denied the existence of 'society' in a telling gaff of the late 1980s; but so too do separate subcultures.

To privilege the whole society over its contentious parts, as the Modernists do, is implicitly to favour the middle class and status quo. This is why Post-Modernists started to ask for an 'inclusive' architecture of contradictions, one that acknowledged social difference as well as the social totality. The high points of this architecture, directed against the exclusivism of Modernity, are not only the buildings of Venturi and his wife Denise Scott-Brown, but Stirling and Wilford's Neue Staatsgalerie in Stuttgart and the hetero-architecture of Los Angeles.

In particular, the eclectic work of Frank Gehry and Eric Moss relates to opposite taste-cultures and differing views of the good life. Gehry's office building in Venice is a key example, combining conflicting architectural languages: high

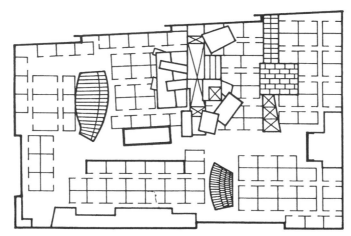

ABOVE and OPPOSITE: Frank Gehry, Chiat/Day/Mojo Office, *Venice, California, 1985-91. An heterogeneity of representational forms – boat, trees, binoculars, fish – and an inclusive language – vernacular, pop, industrial, Post-Modern – are pulled together by self-similarity. The plan, like that of a city, is a collage of monuments and background fabric.*

and low, figurative and industrial, classical and Pop. The pair of binoculars? It is the entrance to the parking garage and the Pop-logo for the advertising agency, in a city full of Flash-Card buildings. The white Modernist boat-image, to the left, is an understated reference to the utilitarian workplace within and the presence of boats in the nearby Pacific, while the copper 'trees', to the right, are sun-shades that service another type of office. The interior space and image change several more times, mediating between old and new, industrial warehouse and cloistered space. Indeed, the complex as a whole has the richness of a small village developed over time. Most tastes and building types are included with no obvious suppressions. One notable benefit of this, in addition to the social pluralism, is the intoxicating ambiguity: one is never sure what building type it is. The environment slips from one category to another, from house to workplace to church to museum to bazaar, and thus a palpable conviviality reigns through-out, as if it really were architecture on a holiday. This category of no-category or all categories is known in Post-Modern poetics as 'the carnivalesque', because it represents an escape from the habitual norms of control.

Another point of this eclecticism – and the architecture of inclusion – is not simply in the multiplicity of the parts but also in the organizational depth with which they are brought together. A structure rich in linkage, with a high degree of redundancy, has organizational depth. I touched on this when describing Coleridge's theory of imagination, which links disparate material to give it depth and richness of meaning. In the Gehry office this depth is created by the trans-formation of themes, by the self-similarity between figural shapes – binoculars, fish-shape, boat-shape, interior monuments – and by the self-similarity of the functional areas – work-stations, stairs, corridors, industrial structures etc. Each

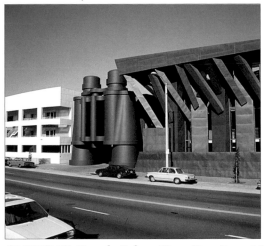

OVERLEAF: Frank Gehry, Vitra Furniture Museum, *Weil am Rhein, Germany, 1987-89. The new vermiform shape-grammar of box-like elements, slightly bent and stacked at disso-nant angles, but harmonized with a continuous surface and colour.*

time we see a similar shape in a new context it gains in depth and resonance. This makes the forms open to multiple interpretation and use. Hence they can change, and resist destructive interpretation.

Gehry's recent shift in architecture, his use of curved forms on boxed volumes, starts with the Vitra Furniture Museum in 1987. This development, which has parallels with Baroque and Art Nouveau architecture and, more particularly, the nearby Expressionism of Rudolf Steiner and Le Corbusier, is different from all these precedents. One is tempted to call it 'vermiform' architecture because it resembles worms. In fact, Peter Eisenman started producing more clearly twisted, linear shapes soon after Gehry's Vitra Museum, inspired by American highways, railroad tracks, spaghetti junctions and the architecture of John Hejduk (see page 140). Worms were in the air. But, again, Gehry's Vitra resists any simple characterization. The shape-grammar is too stubby to be really wormlike, too boxlike to be an animal (unless elephant or whale) and these qualities make it relatively functional and cheap – the attributes of a box.

Here we have a new urban idea, the concept of the single pavilion as a generative form, the notion that the city can be composed of one-room boxes – which Gehry splays at odd angles to give them suspense and tension. This Aggregate Planning, or Collision Composition, is a very effective tool of composition, if it is set off with other types. Both in the Vitra Museum and Factory, and Vitra Headquarters and Center, Gehry has done so.

The Headquarters building contrasts curved-boxes with dumb-boxes. The curves house the more ceremonial meeting place called 'the Villa', while the no-nonsense grids contain the offices. The two systems need each other as anchors and complements, and their scale, material and utilitarian manner fit the mixed context: residential street, motorway and rail track. How typical this site is of our industrial/living landscape. Our urban reality is born mixed and mongrel, utilitarian and sacred. Thus, in both Vitra projects, Gehry contrasts ceremonial and functional space; a particularly apt response to a hybrid progam and site.

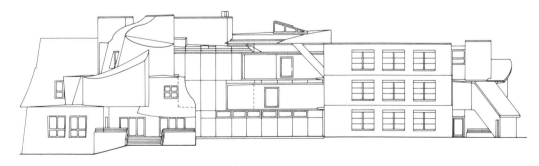

Frank Gehry, Vitra Headquarters, *Birsfelden, Switzerland, 1992-4. Elevation from the north, showing biomorphic villa to the left and rectalinear offices to the right.*

But what happens when a Modernist critic is confronted by these unusual forms? He is thrown off the scent, incapable of understanding what is going on. Modernists want their architecture pure and simplified, repetitive and right-angled, and any deviance from these norms will be severely punished. In the 1960s and 70s the party line was held by the Prime Defender of the Rationalist Faith, Sir Nikolaus Pevsner, with a series of attacks on 'irrationalism', Le Corbusier's Ronchamp, 'Neo-Expressionism', Neo-This and Neo-That.[20] The Puritan-streak in architectural criticism – mostly an Anglo-Saxon hang-up, as the Italians have written – is invariably tied to the commitment to mechanolatry. If you worship the machine you end up with the daft idea that machine-logic should dominate every concern.

Thus it was not surprising that the author of *Theory and Design in the Second Machine Age*, Martin Pawley, became increasingly distraught as Gehry produced ever more curvilinear buildings. In an *Observer* article on the Vitra Headquarters – 'Fall off your chair at the folly' – he damns the complex as 'mad munchkin' architecture, faults the 'tortuously-curved zinc' surfaces for their 'dents and imperfections', explaining that they 'look cheap – which is exactly what they are'.[21]

Actually, what really bothers Pawley is the reverse: his ultimate claim against the building is that 'a great deal of money . . . has been consumed in creating it'. It is both too cheap and too expensive! This is the kind of curved-thinking that Gehry's work sometimes elicits as a Modernist-stock-response. One is reminded of Le Corbusier's three chapters in *Towards a New Architecture* entitled, 'Eyes Which Do Not See'. He was attacking the Beaux-Arts reactionary for not being able to see the new beauty in ocean liners, airplanes and automobiles: the traditionalist was stuck in past stereotypes. Exactly. The same is true of those mired in the Second Machine Age who cannot see the beauty of Gehry's new forms.

Where they see 'mad munchkin' architecture, the open-minded will see a logic of two formal systems, both with their integrity and qualities. For instance, the dented zinc, which unites roof and wall, is a visual texture sought by Gehry in all

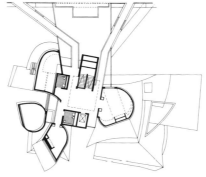

ABOVE and OVERLEAF: Frank Gehry, Vitra Headquarters, *plan and view of the villa. Although shaped, the zinc, tin and plaster forms relate to the mixed neighborhood.*

his sheathed-metal buildings. He is inventing a new well-scaled grammar of curving surface that can overlap, like fish-scales or the hide of an armadillo. The point Pawley cannot understand is that Gehry is seeking a new aesthetic that connects the natural and the built worlds; he is not trying to rebuild the Sixth Machine Aesthetic and getting it wrong. As President Clinton might have reproved Pawley: 'It's not the economy, Stupid; the dents are intentional'.

In any case, the building can defend itself – as I am arguing – because of its organizational depth. It resists any one-liner because it has a series of interlocking meanings which are consistently being transformed. For instance, the floor plan of the Villa shows four basically self-similar forms pinwheeling around a central atrium-space, of similar size, with four basic internal volumes pinwheeling within it. On the exterior, the sculptural room-objects are all gently distorted boxes that are pinched towards the edge, with self-similar punched windows. If there were not these consistent transformations – if the forms were whimsical or solely on the surface or unrelated – then the one-liners would be justified.

Organizational depth can be understood in a literal way as the transformation of the deep structure of the building onto the surface: For example, Gehry's Disney Hall for concerts in Los Angeles, takes acoustic forms and amplifies them on the exterior. The metaphor of music and dance, inherent in the bouncing of sound and light waves, is thus a natural expression for a cultural center, which should make an enjoyable art from forms that seem to grow and move. This building, now under construction, has been damned as 'broken crockery', 'deconstructionist trash' and 'earthquake architecture', as well as being praised as a 'Galleon in full sail', a 'hatbox', and 'growing plant'. [22]

All these metaphors have some relevance, but again the building outdistances them because the forms carry through the whole structure in transformed ways. Because Gehry has used a computer system, borrowed from Dessault Aircraft,

ABOVE and OPPOSITE, LEFT: Frank Gehry, Disney Concert Hall, *Los Angeles, final design, 1993. Block-vermiforms in limestone – computer designed and cut to avoid waste – are broken at the edges to connect with the city and garden. Music, among other functions, has generated the swinging collision of themes.*

to determine the exact shapes, he has been able to cut the curved limestone with minimal loss of material and maximum self-similarity. This would make it a prime example of the Second Machine Aesthetic in Pawley's book, but again this would be like the First Mistake of assuming technology determines form. Gehry's free-form sketches are enough to dispel this idea.

Time and Depth

There is nothing vague in the notion of organizational depth: it can be given a precise numerical description, an equivalent of 'algorithmic complexity theory' (see note 9 and Chapter VI, 'How Much Complexity? – a Cosmic Axiology'). It can be measured roughly by the computer time and cost of a program that reproduces a version of it. Such organizational depth is the basis, I believe, for most appreciation, evaluation and criticism. When someone says a symphony has 'seriousness' or 'integrity', when they impute moral value to a work of art, they are referring in some manner to this quality. When they say a building has 'resonance' or 'deep character', they refer to the internal relations within the architecture, its multivalence. The familiar critical categories of value – unity in variety, transformational consistency, ornamental elaboration, imaginative integrity – illuminate this same area. Formal depth and relationships are ultimately experienced on an ethical plane.[23]

There is a convergence, in experience, of the good, the true and the beautiful. Psychologically speaking, values converge perspectively, at infinity. This is why, when we go as a believer into a great cathedral such as Amiens, aesthetic, religious and cosmic values support, confirm and actually *are* each other. At these rare moments language and value are one. Even atheists will have such a congruent experience if they suspend their disbelief and allow the values to work by analogy. Westerners can appreciate Buddhist temples in just this way.

ABOVE RIGHT: Chartres Cathedral and South Porch, *France, 1194-1260. 'Time is the architect', who carefully builds an organizational depth, in this case inventions in sculpture, structure, stained glass and iconography.*

The case of the great cathedral and Buddhist temple are crucial for understanding organizational depth because they bring up the all important notion of time. If the length of computational time and cost is a crude measure of multivalence or complexity, the reason is that it takes time to make fitting, successful creations – sometimes generations. At Chartres, for many the greatest of the cathedrals, it took something like seventeen building campaigns and one hundred and fifty years of concentrated passion to create the organizational depth.

It is not just the point 'Rome was not built in a day', but the way time *and* a coherently unfolding program were the builders. Change is allowed, but a consistent approach over time builds up quality. The truth that *there is no substitute for transformational time* became obvious in the nineteenth century when the public started comparing the poverty of brand new structures with those that had the rich accretions of the past. Single authorship and a simple program were no substitute for the complex work of creative time. Victor Hugo expressed this view most forcefully in *Nôtre Dame de Paris* as he confronted this great monument of Gothic architecture built over a long period with many changes of style and many anonymous architects:

> Great buildings, like great mountains, are the work of ages. Often art undergoes a transformation while they are pending completion . . . a shoot is grafted on, the sap circulates, a fresh vegetation burgeons. Truly, there is matter for mighty volumes; often, indeed, for a universal history of mankind, in these successive layers of different periods of art on different levels of the same edifice. The man, the artist, the individual are lost sight of in these massive piles that bear no regard of authorship; they are a summation and totalization of human intelligence. Time is the architect – a nation the builder.[24]

'Time is the architect'. There is irreducible truth in this: creative time and destructive time (entropy) are intimately connected by the arrow of time. The longer a house, cathedral or city takes in its design and building, the greater its complexity can be – *if* the architect and client are creatively binding new meanings together. By contrast, fast-food architecture will never have organizational depth. That is why you can consign ninety-five per cent of corporate architecture – by definition – to evaluative oblivion. It does not want to be good, but rather cheap and quick. Positively, it is why there will always be a niche for the individual designer and 'boutique architects' – the ones with small offices who spend years elaborating the inherent meanings they have invented.

A Mozart symphony takes less than a hour to perform, but it is impossible to experience Chartres, appropriately, in less than a day. Some people can take up to a week and the greatest expositor of the building, the Englishman Malcom Miller, gives three-hour expositions on the site, and spends the whole summer, every year, elucidating the depth of meaning built in over time.

Of course, too much time can lead beyond complexity to complication, and many people are quickly bored by what it often leads to: senseless ornament. We immediately feel when an architect pushes beyond this point. Yet, on some occasions, we may even applaud the excess, as with Rococo or High Tech or Eisenmanian architecture. Conversely, if we hate the style, complication gives us a time-honoured prerogative with which to damn it.

It is also obvious that we immediately feel when a building is too simple, raw and without depth. We say it lacks character, or is impoverished. Much of the hostility against the blank, white Modern architecture of the 1920s came from this source, and it prompted Walter Gropius to respond: 'wait for the moss to grow, wait for the buildings to be lived in'. This advice contains the basic truth that time is a builder, and the Modern architects' structures will undergo many changes and improvements as they are inhabited. One owner in Le Corbusier's mass-housing at Pessac changed his house plan six hundred times!

There are simpler solutions. As the Post-Modern injunction has it, 'build-in time through organizational depth'. We can do more than leave it to the moss and the inhabitant, although they are necessary too.

There is nothing more important today than understanding the key role of complexity in the universe. Over time it builds everything we value and love. If we doubt this and are perhaps personally preoccupied, then we have no further to look than the inside our skulls. There it is, the greatest organizational depth in the universe; a trillion synapses carrying millions of weightless and profound thoughts, all due to the build-up of complex structures over eons, and complex emotions over our life-span.

All the marvels of natural and cultural evolution – elephants, Venice and a very good Claret – have long developmental periods, and there may be no short-cuts through the vast stretches of time that it has taken to make them. Some claim that while we can cut down a rainforest in a year, it takes twenty million for it to come back; time is the great organizer. Some claim that it took four billion years to produce us – and it could not have been done quicker or more cheaply, without the pain and learning. In this sense we are built into and out of cosmic time; we are not alienated from the universe, as the Existentialists had it, but are absolute cosmic gestation.

Organizational depth can be seen all around us, in everything we love and look after; but to picture it abstractly we can make use of models developed from network theory. To imagine this, conceive for a moment of a work of art being like an organism with a series of subsystems nested within its overall structure. The linkage of these nested hierarchies, the connections between them, reveal one dimension of how highly organized is the organism. The architectural theorist from Berkeley, Christopher Alexander, has contrasted two different types of organization: the 'semi-lattice' and the 'tree' – the former dense with internal connections, the latter poor in linkage.

Here we have the visual and mathematical analogue of Coleridge's distinction between the synergetic Imagination and the additive Fancy. It is apparent that the great poem or work of architecture forms a tight web of meaning which resists unsympathetic criticism, one-liners, and misunderstandings just as it opens the mind to new interpretation and use. The open work – the *opera aperta* of Umberto Eco – is for the open society and its continual transformation and unfolding.

Organizational depth is one measure of this openness. It is interesting that similar models, or images, have recently been offered as the key to critical value: the lattice, network, labyrinth, and rhizome have become the key images of Post-Modernism, from Umberto Eco's novels to neurobiologists' neural nets. EM Forster's injunction, 'Connect, only connect!' leads to organizational depth, as long as you do not overconnect (which, once again, leads to complication). We will now look at another method for building in organizational depth.

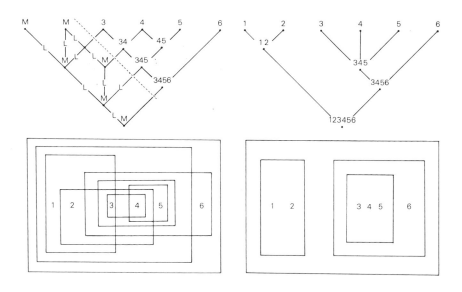

Christopher Alexander, Semi-lattice versus a tree. *Organizational depth, like complexity, depends on the amount and linkage of material. 'More is different'. The number of meanings (M) and links between them (L) are thus a rough measure of organizational depth. Obviously, a simple 'tree' hierarchy has few links but, surprisingly, a structure where everything is linked is also too simple. Both can be described by short algorithms. Thus, between them, the richly connected semi-lattice is highest in organizational depth*

XIV
SUPERPOSITION – CAN ONE BUILD-IN TIME?

In addition to collage, multivalence and folding, what other methods exist for countering the 'depthless present'? Let us return to a major problem of the Modernized, urban landscape.

In the early 1960s, Norman Mailer attacked what was happening in so many American cities: the runaway destruction and development creating 'empty landscapes of psychosis'. The *tabula rasa* created by urban redevelopment reflected and promoted cultural amnesia; Levittown and the planned, instant cities arising in Britain also typified this psychosis. A new anxiety was coined – the 'New Town Blues' – referring to the monoculture that, for so many housewives and young children trapped in the towns, was the daily fare. How, in a purpose-built new city, could one build-in time, cultural variety, and depth?

One method was developed by community architects and those who practiced participatory design. For instance, the Belgian architect Lucien Kroll involves many different participants on the building site, varying from the client to the end-user to the contractors. Even the individual carpenter gets into the act. Each individual and group designs some of Kroll's urban schemes and, thus, they naturally have a variety of style and content absent in the instant city. Also, at the IBA building programme in Berlin, lasting for fifteen years, many different architects provided a related method for reaching a similar variety. Plural design, eclecticism and ad hocism have thus become the main Post-Modern methods for building in organizational depth and the equivalence of time.

In the 1970s Colin Rowe theorized some of these methods as *Collage City*, and the work that resulted – by Venturi, Stirling, Gehry, IBA and Rowe's students – took as its departure point the historic city. The existing urban fabric and layout were privileged as the ground on which new layers were added, or juxtaposed. Hence, the aesthetic of layering, ambiguity, transparency and juxtaposition which became dominant in the 1980s. Hence, Bernard Tschumi's notion of 'super*im*position', making a city plan out of placing one organizational type on top of the existing ground, followed by another and another.

But there is another fairly close method of building-in complexity, which does not privilege the existing fabric. Peter Eisenman, the main protagonist of Superposition, claims it starts with nothing as primary, and tries to bootstrap complexity out of a conjunction of different urban ingredients. A good example is Rem Koolhaas' design for the Parc de la Villette, which superposed five different systems, not favouring one over another. Unfortunately, because it has not been built, we cannot tell if the idea works here, but it is intriguing.

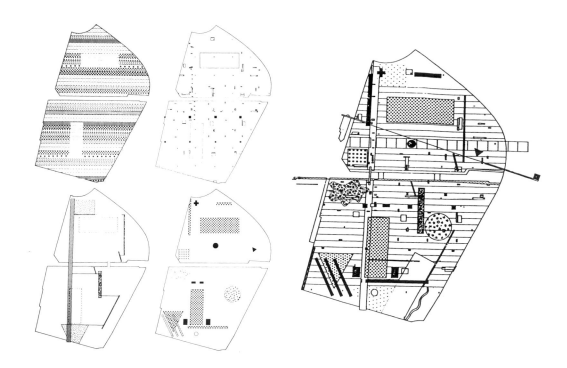

Rem Koolhaas, Parc de la Villette, *Paris, France 1982-3. Various organizational types – bands of planting, confetti of small furniture, circulation and existing buildings – are superposed in rich congestion.*

In effect Koolhaas was a cook who took five ingredients – 1) lateral 'bands' of planting and activity, 2) a sprinkling of randomized small elements called 'confetti', 3) the large elements of the existing site and program, 4) circulation and 5) connecting layers – put them in no apparent order in his soufflé and then hoped they might rise. The lateral bands, so close to each other, provided a new kind of geometric order and would have, if built, provided an extraordinary series of adjacent experiences – rather like a skyscraper tilted on its side, allowing the inhabitants to walk freely from one horizontal floor to another. Even unbuilt, the scheme has had an impact on urbanism and superposition theory, because it shows so clearly the consequences of taking different systems and allowing them to run through and on top of each other *without trying to synthesize or predetermine the interactions*. The reason Eisenman and others hold this proposal in such high regard is that its complex order would seem to emerge *from within* the nonlinear dynamics of the ingredients themselves, not imposed from without.

Ideologically then, superposition is a kind of ultimate democratic method, a bottom-up design where the architect provides the systems, but they do the significant self-organization. Eisenman refers to such design methods as being against 'colonialism', 'fundamentalism' or the male architect's desire to impose his phallocentric will on exterior material.[25] It sounds noble, attractive and worth carrying forward. We can see the basic visual qualities of superposition in Koolhaas' scheme: blurring of categories, adjacent contrasts, one element travelling into another while maintaining its integrity, and great complexity – or is it complication?

There's the rub. As I have mentioned, ecologists who try to create new ecologies which are mature and self-sustaining, find that the order they put the species on the ground, and of course the ground itself, matter a great deal. It is true a new complexity will emerge each time they run the experiment, but it will also be

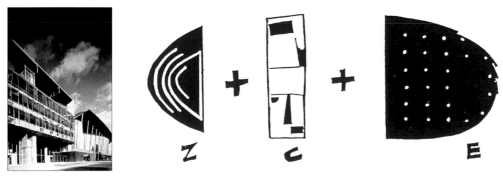

Rem Koolhaas and OMA, Grand Palais, *Congrexpo Lille, France, 1993-4. Ad hoc collision of functions and materials thrown together and wrapped in an ovoid: brute superposition with no attempt at refinement, transition or relationship between parts.*
(KEY : Z= Zenith – 5,500 seats, C= Congress – 3 halls of 1,500, 350 and 500 seats, E= Exposition – 18,000 m²)

79

different depending on the order of the ingredients. By analogy we may suppose that superposition will result, as Eisenman wishes, in a new surprising emergent, which no one has seen – least of all the male architect who has spread his confetti far and wide over the ground. But that surprise is not what the client and society necessarily want of the architect (to which Eisenman might respond: 'too bad, you are interested in control, I am interested in emergence').

Whatever the particular results, it is clear that superposition *is* an alternative to Modernist functional zoning, *tabula rasa* and monoculture. Complexity and time are 'built-into' the approach and we may gauge some of its qualities by looking at Koolhaas' Grand Palais (otherwise titled Congrexpo) at Lille. Here the huge scale of activity has resulted in a statistical relationship of spaces and materials blended together. A leaning polyester wall containing the enormous exhibition space, sits over a giant base of treacly stone holding the parking, and next to a staccato beat of 'broken' windows in front of the mammoth congress halls. According to Complexity Theory, 'big is different', 'more leads to emergent behaviour'.

Another key model for thinking about superposition is the new town proposed by Jeffrey Kipnis, Bahram Shirdel and others at the Architectural Association for an area in China which is undergoing rampant development: the ocean town of Haikou in Hainan province. Kipnis, a friend, sometime-associate and critic of Eisenman, has used several methods of Complexity Theory in the design. No doubt this runaway city in a boiling capitalist economy needs new models of development: its population is projected to mushroom from 40,000 to 400,000 in the next twenty years. Will it look like a western boom-town, mini-Singapore, garbage-dump, sprawl-city or, rather, what combination of them? The question can be posed of many parts of the world undergoing cowboy-growth, free from pollution control.

Kipnis and Co apparently, if I understand their descriptions, have taken their

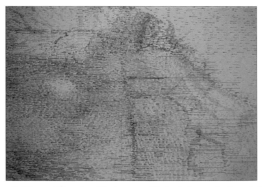

Jeffrey Kipnis, Bahram Shirdel and the AA, Changliu Grouping Area, *Haikou, Hainan, 1994. Original graft (left) and mixed-use drawing (right) resemble a fractal and aerial photograph of a city-region, as well as the authors' concept of an 'urban ocean'.*

first model of urbanism from a beautiful computer graphic – part Pointillist painting, part randomized land-use interaction. This seems an arbitrary model, as all organizational-types have to be, and it does have the virtue of being fresh. It will stimulate new patterns of development not seen before, which of course is why the authors have chosen it. It also has the property of looking like one of those aerial spy photographs used in the Cold War, or now more commonly in the EC to regulate what farmers grow on land. Different crops give off different spectral colours when examined by the French satellite SPOT and, when looked at aesthetically, the coloured polygons resemble some of the best parts of a Seurat canvas. The logic here is that of close-grained diversity, a crazy-quilt of interactions, a mosaic of mixed-use patterns, the very stuff of complexity. Indeed, the computer graphic also resembles the ocean floor with many species living atop each other. Their plan is superposition in action, frozen by camera at an instant.

Carried out in detail, like Koolhaas' design, the scheme layers systems through each other – but a lot more than five. There are the familiar classes of organization such as tourism, industry, university work, agriculture, parkland, roadways, public buildings, and new categories such as 'programmed green' and 'urban ocean' (because of the ocean site): the kind of functional mixtures which might grow in a city of 400,000. These different types are fragmented, spread out and then re-collected in a way which recalls the typical Edge City sprouting up all over the West – as well as their initial generative model, the Pointillist painting.

Another obvious analogy, apparent in their overlay of the four organizational types (Green Network, Urban Ocean, Lot Space and Road Network) is the fractal growth pattern. Here again we could be looking at spy photos, computer-enhanced to bring out the particular element sought. It is appropriate that now such techniques of investigating complex growth (not to mention hidden missiles) are being used to generate cities. They catch the statistical patterns of growing systems: their self-similarity, their fractal nature of spread, their unity in variety, their emergent beauty or, rather, beauty of emergence. They make the new city look as if time has been built into it.

Kipnis calls his initial model the 'original graft' and says the point of a new grafting technique is to make the urban fabric 'vast and coherent, yet capable of sustaining broad formal and programmatic incongruities'.[26] In effect, Shirdel and Kipnis are looking for a method of urban design which will not only make the new city look as if it has evolved rather than been planned, but work in this manner as well.

Their design for the central business district gives us an idea of what the approach looks like in detail. Individual buildings generated by lot division and capitalist development create the typical Modern isolated block, which is then woven into a coherent pattern by self-similar shapes, height lines and the lower buildings and landscape. Like the Rebstock scheme of Eisenman for Frankfurt, we have a hybridization of basically different types: the piloti block and the continuous street building, the transport grid and the organically evolved differentiations of public promenades, gardens and covered markets. The four basic systems – lots, buildings, hard and soft landscaping – are superposed and interlaced. Again, one system is not more primary than, or dominant over, another. This interweaving blurs boundaries, and the folded shape-grammar of some buildings, gardens and roadways makes the new city look even more evolved. The authors speak of 'waves' of landscape and public space 'rippling' through the design, and there are indeed coherent patterns that look as if the movement of water had generated them.

It is a convincing model of the way superposition can provide the organizational depth of a city built over time, and the only obvious questions (besides that of phasing which I have already raised) concern the generic nature of the proposal. It is still an abstract model, rather than a specific design with real institutions and particular buildings. These may come.

Daniel Libeskind has extended the tradition of superposition with his design for the Alexanderplatz in Berlin, which uses a handprint as a generator and then, like Kipnis with his 'grafts', from this initial model he reads out the new implications. But it is Eisenman, theorist of the genre, who has developed it furthest. We will look at the way he uses the method to generate a house based on two soliton waves, and there are schemes going back to 1985 – such as his Romeo and Juliet project – which use superposition to treat thematic issues (the conflict between Romeo's and Juliet's families). So the method can be as much textual and semantic as formal.

Eisenman designed a garden with the Deconstructionist philosopher Jacques Derrida, which is an extreme version of the genre. Their 'Choral Works' for the Parc de la Villette in Paris, masterplanned in the end by Bernard Tschumi rather

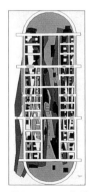 

Kipnis and Shirdel, Changliu Central Business District. *Building, landscaping and public spaces are folded into each other within an oval road network, resulting in variety, close-graining and coherence.*

than Rem Koolhaas, takes superposition towards both complexity and complication. Here is a tilted garden to be made from corten steel, the canted plane representing past, present and future.

Excavations finished in a bright gold – of Paris battlements and an abattoir in Venice – are superposed under and over the tilted plane. These tie the two different cities together, a thematic idea extended by further references which are superposed: L-shaped buildings which Eisenman had designed for Venice and the point grid which Tschumi had used here in Paris. Other binary references include the Paris designer, Le Corbusier, and his project for a Venice hospital, and the typical daily activity in both these cities – digging down and building up

Kipnis and Shirdel, Changliu Master Plan*, superposition of four organizational types (Green network, Urban ocean, Lot space and Road Network).*

on an unstable ground plane. The twisted rhomboid plan, designed by Derrida, represents a lyre and refers to the choral nature of their two voices working for and against each other. With its shifts, collisions and interweavings, it is a lyrical example of superposition which shows that partial identity and order can remain even when so many heterogeneous elements are layered.

It is obviously very complicated, and the gratuity of some of these arcane references can also be questioned: who recognizes the Venice Hospital of Le Corbusier and, if they do, 'so what?' On the other hand, here is an instant palimpsest, the time-city of Rome built in a day, with all that implies. Layers of history scratched down and overlaid, meanings half-forgotten and re-remembered, a density of coherent *and* gratuitous forms. The mind is also like a palimpsest which works through partly remembered fragments and their sudden combinations. So, if the Modern landscape and its urban forces naturally produce cultural amnesia and the depthless present, here is one example of superposition which brings back the notion of layered time to confront the *tabula rasa*. They are both here; neither wins – just like one's mind which has to forget in order to work on its memories.

That each of these unbuilt schemes is *not* an emergent structure goes without saying, since no surprising, holistic behaviour can emerge until the parts are actually functioning. It is to this unpredictable, emergent quality we now turn, in what is one of the most important insights of Complexity Theory, the activity of systems pushed far-from-equilibrium.

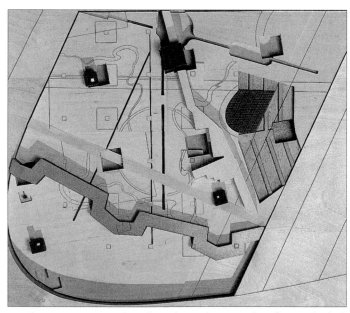

Peter Eisenman with Jacques Derrida, Choral Works, *garden for Parc de la Villette, Paris, 1986. Red pavilions relate to those of Tschumi in the Park, battlements to the history of the site, and other traces to orientation points and the destabilization of life.*

XV

EDGE OF CHAOS AND PURPOSE IN THE UNIVERSE

A key notion of Complexity Theory is that nature, or Gaia, or even the universe as a whole is always pushing itself to the brink, to the boundary between order and chaos. Crisis management is the norm. The End of History, proclaimed by Francis Fukuyama after the end of the Cold War, is not understood by the universe, which has other thoughts, and laws, on its mind. It is always seeking out the tenuous position of maximum choice, maximum computability, where almost any outcome might occur. Creativity is balanced at this knife edge between predictability and randomness. A completely ordered or completely chaotic system is not very valuable because it cannot evolve very far; it cannot improve or progress. By contrast, a system pushed far-from-equilibrium to the boundary between order and chaos – to that crucial phase transition – is rich in possibilities. Chris Langton, one of the founders of Complexity Theory, has discovered analogies of this 'edge' in five different areas.

Dynamical Systems:
Order – '**Complexity**' (Edge of Chaos) – Chaos

Matter:
Solid – '**Phase Transition**' – Fluid

Computation:
Halting – '**Undecidable**' – Nonhalting

Cellular Automata Classes:
I & II – '**IV**' – III

Life:
Too static – '**Life/Intelligence**' – Too noisy[27]

The edge of chaos, depicted on page 36, is a restricted or narrow space which is said to be high in information and computability. This is explained by Chris Langton, in conversation with Roger Lewin, who has written one of the key textbooks on Complexity Theory:

85

'Did you know that cell membranes are barely poised between solid and liquid state? . . . Twitch [one] ever so slightly, change the cholesterol composition a bit, change the fatty acid composition just a bit, let a single protein molecule bind with a receptor on the membrane, and you can produce big changes, biologically useful changes'. I asked whether he was saying the biological membranes are at the edge of chaos, and that's no accident. 'I am, I'm saying the edge of chaos is where information gets its foot in the door in the physical world, where it gets the upper hand over energy. Being at that transition point between order and chaos not only buys you exquisite control – small input/big change – but it also buys you the possibility that information processing can become an important part of the dynamics of the system'.[28]

Because this creative state is so omnipresent and important in the universe, there are inevitably several different models of it, even with matter that looks entirely dead or uncreative. Per Bak, a physicist from the Brookhaven National Laboratory in New York, illustrates the edge condition with his sandpile theory. Imagine a growing sandpile, with sand being continuously funnelled on top of its point until it grows to a certain critical height. We could say the pile is being pushed far-from-equilibrium by the increase in sand – until it starts to collapse. At this stage it has reached 'self-organizing criticality' – the edge of chaos – and its emergent behaviour is holistic, as I will explain shortly. Landslides, or avalanches, of all sizes then occur: a few big ones, more medium ones and lots of little ones.

If you plot these on a graph, you will get what is called 'the power-law distribution' (the general top-left/bottom-right curve), which appears as a constant sign of all systems pushed to the creative boundary point. For instance, in early 1994 the tectonic plates in the Los Angeles basin created very few earthquakes above 5.5 on the Richter scale, quite a few aftershocks between 4 and 5, and over four thousand below 3. Pushed far-from-equilibrium by the energy and compression, pushed to the boundary between order and chaos, the system had maximum computability and creativity of a vicious kind. It was making 'choices'; which is why earthquakes will never be exactly predictable.

Having been in Los Angeles during the 1994 earthquake and aftershocks, and having worked on several landscape mounds, I can vouch for the truth of Bak's propositions. Sand, stones and earth are the ultimate stuff of materialism – yes, Samuel Johnson famously kicked a rock to prove the point – but when they are piled together to a critical point, they suddenly start to act as an organism, all parts communicating with each other holistically. This can be disconcerting if you are used to the mechanical interaction of parts and expect only local failures. In Scotland I pushed a forty-foot snail-shaped mound far-from-equilibrium – producing landslides of all sizes – and then finally built it close to the limit of collapse. Besides inadvertently illustrating Per Bak's point, and the power-law distribution at the edge of chaos, the mound is meant to signify several important things about passage through the site: it is at the culmination of movement through a garden and gives one a view over the landscape, thus satisfying one's curiosity as to the layout and route. Because of its primary role, and because the other garden paths have twists, I have tilted the two paths, so ascent and descent become more difficult.

In Chartres Cathedral a pavement maze is constructed so that the pilgrim is forced to walk away from the goal he is pursuing – Jerusalem, in the center of the maze – in order to achieve it. Once there, he has to face the direction – Jerusalem – he wants to leave. In order to reach the top of the snail-mound I have designed, one has to go up and then down, and in order to leave the top one has to wind down and then up. Who ever said complexity was simple?

The edge between complete order and complete chaos, which is 'complexity' pure and simple, can be characterized in yet other ways that bring out its creativity. Sometimes I am prompted to think of Rem Koolhaas' method of 'panic design', when his creativity results from designing a huge project, or competition, with many variables, moments before it is due. Forcing oneself to the edge of chaos, with maximum information and difference, in a psychological panic, may result in a creativity not otherwise possible. In his case it resulted in his design for Parc de la Villette and The Hague City Hall – both breakthrough projects he might not have produced without being almost too late. Crisis thinking can force through radical solutions. Of course, one has to add the caveat that 'fortune

LEFT: Charles Jencks, Mound, *Scotland, 1992; CENTRE and RIGHT: Rem Koolhaas and OMA,* Library, *Jussieu University, Paris, 1993. Folding sheets create a continuous floor-ramp, a 'warped interior boulevard'. A regular grid of columns, floors, and exterior glass shingles, hold a superposition of urban elements and movements, like the Chiat/Day office.*

favours the prepared mind': without a well-stocked mind balanced at the edge, creativity does not occur. Panic on its own is fruitless.

Another creative design of his, produced under the duress of a big contract (and no time for design) is for a library in Paris. Here, pushed by having to produce a huge library with minimum financing, he suddenly thought of exploiting the fold, a method of design I have already mentioned. Koolhaas folded and cut up sheets of paper and this led him to a new movement system where the library is both a continuous linear route *and* a set of near-horizontal planes. The trick is that much of the library floor has a tilt: not so much that books on a trolley roll away, but just enough to move from floor to floor. In effect, the building is an enormous ramp with various surprising events superposed along the route. The idea has some precedents – the 'architectural promenade' of the seventeenth-century French hôtel, the programmed walk through an English landscape garden, Frank Lloyd Wright's Guggenheim Museum, which also has an organizational ramp as a route of exploration – but Koolhaas' invention is different. He makes the whole floor a ramp and weaves through it a grid of columns and randomized incidents. This, once again, is the method of superposition. Different layers of meaning are strained through each other without any narrative, or priority. This is different from the controlled *promenade architecturale* – for instance Le Corbusier's Mundaneum project – because it refuses to privilege one interpretation over another.

This basic contrast – a continuous path versus inserted event – can also be seen as having a cosmic parallel. On this reading, it is an analogue of contradictory evolution: the way the universe proceeds both by continuous development *and* sudden jumps. Stephen Jay Gould and Niles Eldredge call the combination 'punctuated equilibria'.[29] (Punctuated because the normal, gradual evolution is disrupted by an external event or change in climate).

To return to the general subject, the edge of chaos is really a process, not a static thing like a building; a time-developing quality, not, as architecture is, 'frozen music'. Where Koolhaas conveys the notion through a ramp of movement punctuated by incident, I have represented the idea in a static wall cupboard, with a series of names depicted in vibrating typeface. The shimmering letters are intentionally hard to read; the meanings, as in a puzzle, are meant to be slowly and painstakingly deciphered, because they refer to whole areas of thought, entire world views.

To the left, symbolized by the kitchen clock, are those who believed in a clockwork universe: the Theists and Deists of Modern Christianity such as Newton and his followers, who believed in a deterministic universe (Marx and Freud etc). To the right are their Modernist followers who believed that, ultimately, chance ruled: such scientists as Heisenberg and Monod. Actually, Darwinists, such as the great molecular biologist Jacques Monod, believe that life and evolution can be explained ultimately as the intersection of random mutation and natural selection, or *Chance and Necessity*, as one of his book titles proclaims.

Chance, in this cupboard design, is symbolized by the kitchen dumbwaiter, a sort of roulette wheel. Thus the clock and the roulette-wheel, the determined and random universe (the idea that God is either an absolute dictator, or plays dice with us) are the two extremes which have dominated the world for the last three hundred years. Instead of representing these truths with architectural space, I have used fractured letters and functioning objects, and I have placed in between the polar opposites: those few philosophies, thinkers and scientists who hold a third position. They are given square mirrors to symbolize each individual self and the fact that purpose emerges from the self and defines it (whether it is as small as a single-cell animal or as large as a society).

Why give them central importance? Because in the gap between the two determinisms (chance and necessity), the two most important things in the universe emerge: life and mind. That is why the concept is central in Complexity Theory, and why it is the Holy Grail at the Sante Fe Institute, New Mexico. The theorists there have any number of models that show the great significance of this boundary between very ordered systems and very chaotic ones.

Of course, purpose is denied by doctrinaire Modernists, and disallowed by the Darwinian explanation of evolution. It is the idea that still annoys Richard Dawkins and all those who want their nihilism straight and triumphant. They deny purpose to any but the human world; they do not see goal-directed behaviour going all the way through the universe, but confine it conveniently to the anthropomorphs, themselves. Furthermore, given their Darwinian training, they refuse to see any purpose in the unfolding of cosmic history.[30]

By contrast are those Post-Modernists who believe that the self, the individual

Charles Jencks, Determinism, Purpose, Chance*, Scotland, 1992.*

and self-organizing systems emerge at the important gap between chance and necessity, just at 'the edge of chaos'. Many of them hold the further idea that the universe is unfolding inexorably in a direction of increasing complexity – towards ever more sensitivity and meaning – that history is not just 'one damn thing after another' (as Winston Churchill feared it might be) and that there *is* a new Second Law of Thermodynamics operating, waiting to be formulated. This, if and when it is given adequate expression, may turn out to be the most potent notion of Post-Modernism.

'Teleology without teleology' is the paradoxical way the physicist Paul Davies has expressed the new view. By this he means that the universe is not being driven toward a specific final goal, by one plan or cosmic blueprint, the ancient idea of teleology, but that it does have a predisposition to go in certain directions – and life and increasing complexity are two of them.[31]

Similar conclusions have been drawn by those scientists who favour the anthropic principle, who see in the constants of nature a predisposition for development in certain favoured directions. This idea of predisposition rather than predeterminism is compatible with the notion of the edge of chaos, because it features free will and choice as essential elements of open systems. Many similar conclusions have been drawn by those connected with the Santa Fe Institute: Doyne Farmer, Norman Packard, Stuart Kauffman *et al.* While teleology and vitalism have been banished by Modernist reductivism, the predispositionist framework may well become an orthodoxy in ten years. To invoke the theory about the theory, one might say some of the best minds are balanced at this creative edge.

Stuart Kauffman finds all living systems aiming at the edge of chaos: the points of maximum aggregate fitness where the local ecology and the individual are both pushed to their best interactive limit. This notion of progress deep within nature echoes throughout history, from Aristotle to those ecologists who believe in 'climax ecology'. And this naturally brings us to the complicated relations between the planet's ecology – Gaia – and the modern economy.

XVI
ECOLOGICAL CHALLENGE AND SPECIES EXTINCTION

The sceptical reader must be wondering at this point: 'If the universe is progressing, why are things getting so much worse?' It is a basic question, a childlike question, and the better for that. How can nature be evolving towards more complexity, ever higher levels of organization *and* our earth be evolving towards ever greater levels of eco-catastrophe?

Almost everyone knows the litany of doom; it has been standard since Professor Paul Ehrlich's best-selling *The Population Bomb* (1969), which has sold over three million copies. The world's population has grown by more than 1.9 billion since that time, and added a host of other well-known problems to that of mass-starvation: the hole in the ozone layer, acid rain, global warming, the depletion of topsoil and many other resources on which we, and life, depend. The crisis is real. Earth summits and Population summits are devoted to it, as well as efforts from almost all of the political spectrum.

At the same time, there has been another story going on that is just as real: the world economy has been booming for the last fifty years, achieving growth levels, particularly in Asia, which are unprecedented. As an editorial in the *Washington Post* put it:

> During the past half-century the greatest changes in the terms of life on this planet have been driven by astonishing rapid economic growth. For the first time, it has not been limited to one region or a few countries. The rise in wealth in the late 20th century has been more sustained and more widespread than ever before in history . . . Economic growth is measured in dollars, but it translates into other and much more important things – better health and longer lives, less harsh physical labour, greater economic security.[32]

Although this statement exaggerates the extent of economic wellbeing, it does represent the optimistic views of the United States Establishment: the *Washington Post* is probably a good index of what the major economic thinkers at the World Bank, IMF, and the White House are hoping in their buoyant moments (when they do not remember the unfortunates made worse off by development).

Obviously both the economic and ecological stories have some truth, and certainly they are both connected, because the economy depends on the world's ecology, or Gaia. It is also clear that both stories are in conflict and that we do not have a method to measure, or deal with, this. There is no way, at present, to put in a balance-sheet the opposite goals, or discourses. How can one weigh the suffering of the two billion (or so) poorest inhabitants of the world, whose misery is partly caused by development elsewhere, with the economic success of the billion (or so) who are bettering themselves? What about the several billion who have stayed relatively stationary, and what about the 5,000 different languages in which to take such polls? Even if there were a measure, would the Modernist method of pricing be the right one? If a common measure were put on all things, it would come to that – some measure of the world's gross product.

Take the famous $1,000 bet that Paul Erhlich and Julian Simon, the economist, made in 1980: it epitomized the two discourses, often called the 'doomsters' versus the 'boomsters'. Erhlich, the doomster, responded to a challenge by Simon to let anyone pick any natural resource – grain, coal, timber, oil, metals – and any future date. If the resource grew scarcer, as the population grew, then the price would rise, but if the cost went down, then the resource would be plentiful (or a substitute would have been found). Ehrlich and his group bet on five metals – chrome, copper, nickel, tin and tungsten – and in 1990 the wager was due. Just as Simon predicted, because of gains in technology and human inventiveness (that is, indirectly because of population growth), the price of these resources had declined. Once again, *homo economicus* had beaten *homo ecologicus*, at least in the short term; as for the long term – well, 'in the long term, we are all dead', as they say.

Or do they? It is not so simple as any wager or discourse would have it. As most traditional societies argue, one invests for children and friends as well as society and the land generally – for sustainability – and both economists and ecologists are adopting the catch-all 'sustainable'. As even the quote from the *Washington Post* demonstrates, 'sustainable growth' is the phrase of left and right; but it means different things to different people. In Russia, for instance, the average life expectancy for men has dropped from the high sixties to fifty-nine years; about the same is true in Pakistan.[33] That is not 'sustainable', any more than the pollution levels now caused by economic growth in China are. Everywhere Modern success is killing the planet – yet no society wants to give it up. The related paradox can be put succinctly: there are more people better off than ever before in human history, and more people worse off – partly because there are many more people. The population bomb is in the shape of a trumpet of growth, and that trumpet includes the growth of opposites. This sustains the two discourses, allows them to be selective with statistics and talk past each other. It also means they miss a possible common ground: *a third model of restricted growth* and the preservation of much of nature.

At the same time another discourse is not being heard: that of the other species. According to the best estimates of the best scientists, as summarized by EO

Wilson, every year some 27,000 species of plant and animal are becoming extinct – that is seventy-four a day, or three an hour.[34] In fifty years, at this rate, all the known species will have disappeared, and the only solace is that we will have discovered a lot more (assuming we are not one of the disappeared). Much of this extinction is not intentional, but caused by destruction of physical habitat. It is simply a by-product of the Modern model of economic success, an 'invisible hand' that Adam Smith could not divine because, in his period, the economy, relative to the ecosphere, was not so gigantic.

If we are honest with this evidence and put it in historic context, it appears we are at the beginning of the sixth major mass-extinction in earth's history. The previous five took about seventy per cent of the species with them, except the Permian/Triassic, which may have taken ninety-five per cent.[35] By the year 2000, estimates are that we will have inadvertently killed between ten and twenty per cent of species. Not a year goes by without a warning that the most loved and admired species – the tiger, whale, rhino, cheetah and elephant – will end up confined to zoos. Only a very few, like Julian Simon, still take a sanguine view of this and challenge the evidence.[36] The rest of the experts, by and large, understand that we are already well into a period of mass-extinction.

The ramifications for architecture, as for everything else, are alarming, but there is a danger in focusing too exclusively on the alarm. Like all threats to life – nuclear war, world depression, disease, being hit by an asteroid – it can easily become obsessive and turn into another single issue to dominate all concerns. At the same time, it seems to me, species extinction and ecological destruction will form the background for cultural discussion during the next hundred years, as the Third and Fourth Worlds struggle to modernize. Perhaps they can be persuaded to follow new models but, at present, Western modernization is their dominant goal. The economic imperative they face from the global market – IMF, GATT and World Bank – will keep the ecological crisis hot for the foreseeable future. What then are the implications for architecture?

XVII
GREEN ARCHITECTURE

To raise the question of architecture in a context of species extinction is to go from the cosmic to the provincial, and yet all professions face the same problem: they are tiny actors on a global stage. In coming to terms with this central issue, architecture is like any discipline. The first point to be made is depressing: in thirty years of designing ecological houses and emphasizing responses to environmental problems, individual architects have *achieved relatively little.* The problems dwarf their efforts, grow exponentially faster than any solutions, and what the conscientious ones usually have to show for their concern is a list of client rejections. The environmental issue may have been on the social agenda, but it often comes second to economic imperatives.

The second point is only somewhat less upsetting, and shows that architects do not have the real power to change important aspects of the problem: the greatest gains for ecology, dwarfing all others, could probably be made by living in mud huts or, better, underground. At a minimum, architects could be most effective by simply doubling the insulation in every building and siting them ecologically (that is, with most of the windows to the south in temperate climates and to the north in hot climates). Most of our energy and pollution problems, architecturally speaking, are caused by heat-loss and gain, and if we could solve this problem the rest would be minor. The servicing of buildings is probably responsible for half of the world's fossil fuel consumption. Since architects design at best five per cent of world building, and probably much less than one per cent, it becomes clear that the problem is in the hands of politicians and developers, and those who can enforce laws dealing with insulation.

The last, potentially depressing point is that good ecological building *may* mean bad expressive architecture: in the trade-off between these two competing concerns, it often makes more eco-sense to push the building down, pack it tight and minimize surface. A blob, or at least an igloo-shaped mass trying to burrow underground, is where eco-logic leads. This, of course, is potentially interesting at the level of surface articulation – we are even beginning to see an emergent, interesting blob-architecture – but it *does* sacrifice the elaboration of free space.

For such reasons I will leave a full discussion of the political and energy issues to others, and concentrate on an architecture that delights in the ecological paradigm for its philosophy of holism, its style, and the way it illuminates the complexity paradigm. For those who wish to know how an ecological city might function I recommend Curitiba in Brazil, where the mayor has made the difference by introducing public transport, social housing, and a host of other policies such as 'recycling as a religion'. For those who are interested in social responsibility and building eco-villages, there are the countless examples of urban villages being supported by Prince Charles, designs by Duany and Plater-Zyberk, and books: Peter Katz's *The New Urbanism, Towards an Architecture of Community* (1994), and Peter Calthorpe, *The Next American Metropolis: Ecology, Community, and the American Dream* (1993). There are a number of books on green architecture by authors such as Brenda and Robert Vale; good individual buildings by Team Zoo in Japan, Ken Yeang in Malaysia, countless German architects including Gunther Benisch, and the great number of American self-builders. The tradition of individualist-ecologists has not diminished since Thoreau.

Now that the American Institute of Architects has adopted ecology as an official part of its programme, and a World Congress of Architects, attended by fourteen thousand, has signed a *Declaration of Interdependence* concerning the environment, we can expect to see quite a few more environmental regulations, with the whole issue becoming mainstream.[37] Increasingly the media, young students, politicians and much of the general public are becoming knowledgeable about the crisis, so it is possible that some catalytic event – or catastrophe –

James Wines and SITE, Covered Walkway – Cooling System, *Expo 92, Seville, 1992. Earth, air, water and sun are dramatized in this snake building.*

will trigger a sufficient response. As we await such a shift, it is essential to cultivate a tradition of sensuous, creative Green Architecture – one based on the new sciences of complexity. Otherwise there is the danger of architectural and psychological burn-out, as young architects and environmentalists see their work overwhelmed by much larger economic forces, and are reduced to a functionalist response and moralistic protest. Such a tradition is only just starting.

The work of the group called SITE is foremost among architects expressing the artistic potential of ecology. Led by James Wines, this team of artists and designers has always produced site-specific architecture, as its name implies. Their projects transform the local conditions, especially climatic and geological ones. Thus buildings tunnel beneath the ground or have the ground plane lifted to run over their top; they show the local earth, water and vegetation in cross-section by putting it behind glass and thereby drag a didactic art out of eco-realism. A case in point is their work at Expo 92 in Seville. Their communication corridor that linked pavilions performed a very welcome service in the sweltering heat – it brought the spray of mist, smell of plants, coolth of flowing water, shade from the sun and delight to the eye, by undulating in surprising ways. The drama of a water-wall, *sweating* its way around a meandering site, was turned into a witty comment on the four elements. On one side you are in shade and relative darkness, beside an outdoor restaurant with the mist wafting gently over your head. Then you walk through the water-wall into the glare of Sevillian sun which cuts you dead. You look down to see a little river meandering by the glass wall, take in the cross-section through the pebbles, topsoil and growing vegetation – the eye travels up until it reaches the roof garden protection, blue sky and . . . monorail! It all makes sense as Expo-Ecology (a contradiction in terms); a perfect comment on the fundamental conflict of our time.

For the Tennessee Aqua Center in Chattanooga, near the famous TVA authority which turned water into electric power during the 1930s, SITE has extended their ironic and delightfully functional art. This proposal also has undulating walls, with ground and growth penetrating above, below and through them.

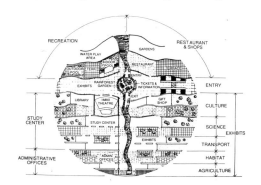 

James Wines and SITE, Tennessee Aqua Centre, *Chattanooga, Tennessee, 1993.*

96

nistic and out of place – especially at Expo 92 in Seville. Here the Hungarian Pavilion could only be called religious in the sense that 'Woolworth Gothic' was called sacred when the world's tallest 'cathedral of commerce' was built in 1915: an adman's joke on Christianity.

No matter; sited sensitively, Makovecz's pulsating roof-forms can survive these infelicities because they are creative openings in the language of architecture; they extend the shingled, layered skin-building. By rotating structural forms slightly and then finishing them with overlapping flat planes, he has opened up a very fruitful grammar of Organic Architecture in wood. This has implications for cosmogenic architecture in showing the possibilities of a rolling, wave-form structure punctuated by folds.

Significantly, Makovecz sees the organic tradition in ecological and cosmic terms. For him it includes not only the canonic figures – Frank Lloyd Wright, Bruce Goff, Herb Greene, Lechner Odon, Kos Karoly, Rudolf Steiner, Antonio Gaudi and William Morris – but a response to the environmental crisis in Europe: acid rain, Chernobyl and runaway economic development. As for Wright *et al*, Makovecz writes:

> . . . it is the *mode of thinking* or their *view of life* which makes these people representatives of organic architecture. One of the significant things about this view is that they are searching for metaphors between the meta-

Anton Alberti and Van Hunt, MV, NMB Bank, Amsterdam, 1984-87. Ten cores snake around the site in masonry and, with passive solar heating, make this energy efficient, fractured expressionism.

Indeed gardens flow in lines through the structure, as if the building were a round valve placed in a stream – hence the undulations, hence the omnipresent metaphor of water which cascades through the building uniting the central rainforest garden to the different 'narrative environments' and a massive waterfall. While the architects speak of the building's cosmic symbolism – the circular form suggesting ancient ceremonial worship of the sun, moon, and heavens – what strikes me is its similarity in plan to a living cell: the nucleus, of course, where the DNA would be stored, is an information center nurtured by the rainforest garden, the Eden of ecologists. Many such mappings between living process and building are suggested, so the symbolism underlines the programmatically green functions such as energy saving, recycling and the choice of environmentally sympathetic materials.

The most unlikely candidate for the most ecologically-responsive building in England is the large, rambling De Monfort University School of Engineering in Leicester. Labelled Post-Modern Gothic, given a pedigree that extends back to the Gothic rationalism of Pugin and Viollet-le-Duc, and with gables, pinnacles, pointed arches and polychromatic brickwork, it projects an image which is anything but environmentally sensible. As often, the stereotypes are wrong, especially those which associate efficiency and low cost with minimalist, white cubes. The building simply does not look like any engineering building since 1875. The architects, Alan Short and Brian Ford, have achieved a tight-packed village scale which is very energy-efficient in a traditional way.

It is the form and fabric of the building, according to an environmental report,

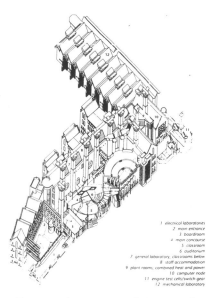

1 electrical laboratories
2 main entrance
3 boardroom
4 main concourse
5 classroom
6 auditorium
7 general laboratory, classrooms below
8 staff accommodation
9 plant rooms, combined heat and power
10 computer node
11 engine test cells/switch gear
12 mechanical laboratory

Alan Short and Brian Ford, De Monfort School of Engineering, *Leicester, 1991-93. Traditional and contemporary means of energy saving.*

that achieves the savings in fuel.[38] Since engineering studies generate intense heat and light, this can be recirculated, and since the overall building is broken up into a lot of small, top- and side-lit volumes, natural light can be bounced around in a very efficient way. Mechanical cooling has been eliminated by the use of deep reveals, the very visible roof stacks (which draw air through the entire building) and a central four-storey concourse constructed with a masonry mass that maintains a stable temperature: cool in summer, warm in winter. Surprise, surprise, all of these are traditional methods that architects have forgotten – or learned to dislike – when fossil fuel became cheap.

But it is the confident, exuberant use of these means that gives the building character. Gable-forms are transformed around the site – pointed, triangular, splayed, staggered – and ten different window-forms are used. Self-similarity and fractals appear again, played against a stable background of ruddy brick, and made more stable because the mortar is coloured to match the brick. The results are *not* so much Neo-Gothic Revival as Neo-Queen Anne Revival; the shingle gables and white trim prove that as much as the consistent asymmetrical symmetry. Nevertheless, I do not believe any historical labels do justice to the synthetic thinking behind the building, which borrows as much from the contemporary pavilion-planning of Frank Gehry as the tradition of thin industrial structures. This is a robust architecture that resists easy interpretation, showing that hallmark of Complexity evaluation: the quality of organizational depth.

Today's 'ecologically correct' building has an affinity with the Organic and Expressionist traditions of architecture, which were marginalized by Modernism earlier this century. Anton Alberts, and his group in Holland, has combined these two traditions at the NMB Bank on the outskirts of Amsterdam in producing what is often called the greenest architecture, or 'the lowest energy-consumption building in the world'. Passive solar heating, small windows, the stack-effect, centralized courts, masonry mass – the usual means seem to work. Here the fractal geometry of the transformed pentagon breaks up a huge mass and yet the scheme still feels massive – unlike the Leicester building. This is caused by the old Modernist disease I have mentioned – 'monothematatis' – that is, 3.5 million bricks, and the absence of scaling devices at different levels.

Another exponent of Organic Architecture who synthesizes traditions which were marginalized earlier this century is the Hungarian Imre Makovecz. He combines the National Romanticism prevalent in 1900 with folk architecture, underground green building, and anthropomorphic or zöomorphic metaphors. Because of the latter, his work is closest to a recognizable green architecture connected to nature. Faces, eagles, lips, eyes, skin, torso and muscles bulge out from his undulating shingles. The explicit symbolism, especially when it is crowned by religious spires and crosses, tends to backfire because it is anachronistic and out of place – especially at Expo 92 in Seville. Here the Hungarian Pavilion could only be called religious in the sense that 'Woolworth Gothic' was called sacred when the world's tallest 'cathedral of commerce' was built in 1915: an adman's joke on Christianity.

No matter; sited sensitively, Makovecz's pulsating roof-forms can survive these infelicities because they are creative openings in the language of architecture; they extend the shingled, layered skin-building. By rotating structural forms slightly and then finishing them with overlapping flat planes, he has opened up a very fruitful grammar of Organic Architecture in wood. This has implications for cosmogenic architecture in showing the possibilities of a rolling, wave-form structure punctuated by folds.

Significantly, Makovecz sees the organic tradition in ecological and cosmic terms. For him it includes not only the canonic figures – Frank Lloyd Wright, Bruce Goff, Herb Greene, Lechner Odon, Kos Karoly, Rudolf Steiner, Antonio Gaudi and William Morris – but a response to the environmental crisis in Europe: acid rain, Chernobyl and runaway economic development. As for Wright *et al*, Makovecz writes:

> . . . it is the *mode of thinking* or their *view of life* which makes these people representatives of organic architecture. One of the significant things about this view is that they are searching for metaphors between the meta-

Anton Alberti and Van Hunt, MV, NMB Bank, Amsterdam, *1984-87. Ten cores snake around the site in masonry and, with passive solar heating, make this energy efficient, fractured expressionism.*

Imre Makovecz Studio, Jim Gomez and Prince of Wales Institute, Spitalfields Shelter, *London, 1994. Seven-sided roof structure with layered and rotated clapboards, the roof both like a dome and undulating in a direction, like an animal.*

nature of society and the created world. The abyss which opens again and again between these two is unbearable for them. To this end, Gaudi and Morris used plant metaphors, Greene used animal metaphors and Rudolf Steiner used human metaphors. It was absolutely essential for these architects to view the world as a continuity.[39]

This is true. The greater tradition of Organic Architecture has always tried to resolve the contradictions between nature and culture, and seen culture in cosmological terms. Makovecz himself is drawn to 'the cultures of ten, twenty thousand years ago', to the archetypes of Carl Jung and to the two great ancient cultures of Central Europe, the Celtic and the Scythian. Hence his work has a basic, primitive embeddedness in place, a fundamental spirituality that relates to the earth and the animism of Old Europe.

To invoke the idea of 'Old Europe', in this context, is to bring up the question of the agrarian culture that stretched from England to the steppes of Russia for 5,000 years, from 8,000 to 3,000 BC. This neolithic civilization was matrifocal, art-loving, and thrived peacefully in unfortified settlements. According to archaeologist Marija Gimbutas, who coined the term 'Old Europe', this goddess-worshipping culture was invaded by nomads from the steppes, who worshipped a sky-god and were 'indifferent to art'. They came, like Genghis Khan's hordes four thousand years later, speeding in from the East on horseback – marauding, pillaging and, after several invasions, intermarrying. The older world view, honouring the fecundity of the earth as symbolized by women's sexuality and reproduction, was replaced by a patriarchical-chieftain social system that desacralized the earth.[40] New Europe, with few exceptions, has continued this pattern.

Inevitably, archaeologists and anthropologists, especially some males, have questioned this view, but the archaeological evidence – and now the historical genetic evidence – seems to confirm it.[41] In the nature of the case, until a 5,000 year-old man tells us in writing it will never be definitely proved. But the more we analyze the pottery, many female images, village layouts (no fortifications, no arsenals), and burial conventions (women given equal or slightly elevated status to their husbands), the more we look at the population genetics of successive invasions crushing Old Europe, the more probable the theory becomes. Simply put, it is this: the figure we call 'Gaia', the pre-Greek name for Mother Earth, *was* a cultural focus for 5,000 years prior to the current focus, Father God. Old Europe enjoyed peace and the arts; New Europe prefers war and money.

That is a bald way of putting it, without any qualifications or archaeological hedging, but this book is a polemic; we are looking at the big picture. The interested reader can easily follow up the controversy; it is as wide and deep as that over the Gaia Hypothesis itself, to which we now turn.

XVIII
GAIA – IS SHE TELEOLOGICAL?

The idea that the earth is alive and is a superorganism with a will of its own is common to many ancient cultures. Giving this personification a woman's name, Mother Earth, or the pre-Greek 'Gaia', makes explicit the animistic metaphor – that all of nature, including nature as a whole, is ensouled. Inevitably Modern science threw out this 'pathetic fallacy' reducing the living world to the mechanistic interaction of particles and dead matter. It saw life simply as some unknown complication of basically dead stuff.

From time to time, various ecological thinkers – in the eighteenth century the Scottish physician and farmer James Hutton, in the nineteenth the Austrian geologist Eduard Suess, and in the early twentieth the Soviet physicist Vladimir Vernadsky – put forward the notion that the earth was a superorganism. They invented concepts, such as the 'biosphere', which explained how it worked, but their basic concept was never taken up because mainstream science, the Modern paradigm, was against it.[42] How could earth be alive? Can she think, plan, have offspring, and regulate her affairs? In short, is she purposeful, teleological? No, impossible! The concept is rubbish.

It was not until 1972 that James Lovelock, an atmospheric chemist and inventor, pondered views of the earth seen from space and saw just how unusual this 'blue planet' was compared to all other ones. Soon thereafter his concept of Gaia came into strong focus. Along with the microbiologist Lynn Margulis, he formulated what could be called the 'Robust Gaia' theory: 'Life, or the biosphere, regulates or maintains the climate and the atmospheric composition at an optimum for itself'.[43] This is nearly teleological and the evidence was, and is, overwhelming: for the last 3.8 billion years the superorganism – or interlocking systems of life, physical conditions and chemical composition – has kept a host of important dynamics just right for her prosperity. According to this hypothesis, she has cybernetically regulated moderate levels of salt in the oceans, maintained the relative constancy of climate and, most impressively, kept oxygen where it needs to be for life – around twenty-one per cent of gases – over several million years.

Could these things be a happy accident of finely-tuned coincidences? Or had God created earth and set the levels of carbon dioxide, methane, nitrogen, and oxygen in just the right proportions? If so, had He patiently stood by and regulated them every time He struck earth with an asteroid, wiping out seventy-five per cent of life? Either He is in charge, or not; and if not, what is? Natural selection? But there are *not* a billion other planets, varying their gaseous conditions and having offspring to select from, so that the most fit survive. Therefore it cannot be that Darwinian mechanism. No, the eloquent facts of the finely-tuned, finely-maintained earth ask to be explained and, if it is not a miracle, what is it? Whatever one thinks of the Gaia Hypothesis, some version of it must be true.

Lovelock's more recent formulation, in 1991, could be called the 'Modest Gaia' theory: 'The modern expression of James Hutton's superorganism, Gaia, is the Earth seen as a single physiological system, an entity that is alive at least to the extent that, like other living organisms, its chemistry and temperature are self-regulated at a state favourable for life'. [44] The main difference between what I call the Robust and Modest versions is the shift from being alive to being 'systems', and the qualifier – 'alive to the extent' of favourably regulating earth's conditions for life itself. Modern scientists have been unremitting in their attacks on Lovelock, because they hate the whiff of teleology, and hence, have forced him to tone down the stronger version many times. Yet still it grows back, as hardy as Gaia herself.

Trees make rain, especially in the rainforest; clouds form over the ocean to let through the right amount of sunlight; and a thousand other living and non-living systems experience positive and negative feedback to keep gases at the correct proportion: just explosive enough to make Gaia metabolize but not burn up. With a team of artists, I have constructed a model of Gaia which shows some of these interactions over the earth's four billion years.

Reading down from the top we can see the early, dead planet, then the origin of life 3.8 billion years ago, then the very important 'tight coupling' between the three main players: life, chemical compositions and physical conditions (represented by the three undulating metals). The structural members on the four sides show how Gaia pumped down carbon dioxide from, roughly, a deadly twenty per cent of atmosphere to its present low of 0.03 per cent (today, unfortunately, rising and creating the 'Greenhouse Effect'). Methane is shown falling and levelling out, oxygen rising up to its crucial twenty-one per cent and nitrogen balanced as the major gas. Two more important events are shown, one of them a continuous process, the other a punctuation: at the bottom of the model sun rays flare out and increase the temperature of the earth, over four billion years, by twenty-five per cent.

But, miracle upon miracle of Gaia, although the sun *has* become that much hotter, the earth's surface has not – because the temperature is regulated by the planetary system as a whole. Secondly, the five major mass-extinctions can be seen, depicted as if each were the result of a comet or asteroid hitting the earth. The cause may have been volcanoes or it may, more simply, have been self-organizing tendencies in the whole system – the way populations can suddenly die off because of chaotic forces built into the cycles.

Charles Jencks, Gaia, Scotland 1994 (constructed by Brookbrae). The history of the earth represented as a spiral of interacting forces. The snake-like bands show the tight coupling of life with physical and chemical elements, all working together for the benefit of life. The circular supports represent gases pumped up or down by Gaia; sun rays come up from the base, holding up the whole system, and explosions – mass extinctions – punctuate the spiral route.

Lovelock and many Gaians, however, do not see this developing catastrophe as the end of Gaia – far from it. The earth system is too robust to be killed by us, by a million hydrogen bombs, or their equivalent in one of the asteroid explosions earth has received. There is some solace in knowing that if *homo sapiens* does not prove wise enough, and is snuffed out by Gaia as she jumps to a new level of self-organization, at least life will go on and a new robust history will start. This view of nature and history has some optimism and dignity to it. As the 'geologian' Thomas Berry emphasises: the earth is primary, we are secondary, and if we continue to deny this simple fact and go on as we are, we will go the way of the dinosaurs. That will be a kind of cosmic Last Judgement by Gaia.

In such ways we find morality and ethics built into the universe. Ecological harmony – synergy, co-operation, symbiosis – were working away long before we transformed them into systems of judgement, customs, or laws. The same is true for other affective qualities – love, beauty, and aesthetics – they pre-date us and exist independently of us. Such notions are, of course, anathema to the Modernists, who claim that all beauty is in the eye of the beholder and all morality is socially constructed. But before taking on these points in the conclusion, we should deal with that other question which annoys them: teleology. This can be seen in the argument over 'ecological succession': do ecologies grow and progress according to a fundamental pattern or do they change any-which-way?

There is evidence to support both views. The classic position was put forth in the nineteenth century and then developed in the early twentieth by Frederick Clements. An ecosystem, he argued, develops in a series of stages, from initial 'pioneer' to mature 'climax', and this final stage has maximum stability, diversity and robustness – like Gaia herself.[45] Just as the individual embryo grows and passes through several stages, largely according to a plan laid down in its genes, so an ecosystem progresses from level to level. This idea of a clear progression, through what Clements called a 'sere' to a monoclimax, was criticized eventually by showing that an ecosystem could have several different outcomes of development. There was no single, deterministic line.

Furthermore, as more ecosystems were studied, the distinction between climax and successional communities became less clear; nature seemed to be in constant flux. The argument continued through the 1960s as Eugene Odum answered these criticisms with a more sophisticated model of development: one that used twenty-four indices, contrasting early with mature stages. For instance, a mature ecosystem is good at nutrient conservation whereas a pioneer one is poor; a well-developed ecosystem has narrow specialization whereas a young one is broadly focused. A rainforest, for instance, is stable, low in entropy and high in information whereas one which has been cut back has the reverse qualities. These tendencies are shared across different ecosystems and they form, according to Odum, the unifying principle of the science of ecology.[46] Using this principle, one knows if an ecosystem is flourishing or declining. Without it one can do what one likes, including developing the ecosystem for economic use.

This is where theory supports, or contradicts, ideology. It is predictable that 'free-market-ecology', the dominant model, resists any teleology in nature and emphasizes the random flux of ecosystems – which, as it happens, they also show. 'Boom and Bust May Be the Norm in Nature' announced a headline in the science section of the *New York Times* on March 15, 1994. The evidence comes once again from the population dynamics illuminated by Chaos Theory. The computer model showed that instability and change are the rule for such animals as the Dungeness crab: there is no climax and no stability or maturity as far as its cycles of population are concerned. If ecosystems are simply the sum of all these random fluctuations, then they too must show ultimate chaos.

Yet the point is that ecosystems are not the sum of the species; rather they are holistic, and emergent wholes at that, not wandering species which boom and bust. They may show a variety of outcomes in developing, but they also go through a series of directional stages that aim at greater diversity to achieve greater stability. The more the variety, the more choice the system has, then the sturdier its response, usually, to exterior insults. Like Gaia, the goals of this directional process are robustness and survival.

So, after all, there is teleology, if we consider predisposition rather than a single, final outcome which is the goal. Ecosystems and Gaia are 'trying' to evolve towards greater complexity, and ever higher and more stable levels of organization, like the rest of the universe. There is telos in Gaia as it pushes the interacting variables of chemistry, physical conditions and life to their limit, but this is not a 'life force' or 'vital fluid' in the sense argued by the Vitalists. Rather, it is the emergent property of all properties.

The importance of this general principle suggests why the two books of 1992 on Complexity Theory, by Lewin and Waldrop, were subtitled variously 'life on the edge of chaos' and 'the emerging science at the edge of order and chaos'. To be balanced near or on this edge is to have maximum choice and creativity. It sounds precarious and, as mentioned, the edge might be pictured as very thin – like the ocean surface between water and air – but, like the ocean, it is also nearly infinite in extent.

If we return briefly to architecture and urbanism, and try to imagine the analogues of this powerful edge, they might be the robust building or urban village, one with maximum order and chaos, one with maximum diversity and life, one that could withstand the greatest amount of 'insults' (pollution, development, mixed use, and multiple interpretation). No doubt Georgian terrace housing is robust on some of these levels and it has, after all, survived many changes in use. I have in mind a more complex structure, with further differentiations: something between Le Corbusier's Unité d'Habitation, the 1960 megastructure, and Jane Jacobs' urban village. The interior of Frank Gehry's office building, which we looked at, is something like that: an office that is at once a village of avenues and streets, a commercial place, a church and a domestic building. Here we find complexity, ambiguity, old uses, new functions, multiple meaning and a very sensuous work environment – a veritable rainforest of architecture. Of course, a built environment can become too complex, and hence, a complication, but the Gehry office is one standard which stops short of this creative edge.

To summarize, we might conclude that a mature, homeostatic structure is the goal of Gaia, and therefore should be the goal of architecture. But is it that simple? In 1992 I visited James Lovelock in his Cornwall retreat, surrounded by a regenerating growth he had planted to test his theories and to keep intruders, like me, at bay. He was working on several computerized models that showed, if I understood them rightly, that Gaia could get tired and bored. If she were never perturbed but continued on recycling in the same old way, year after year, she could sink into the equivalent of a 'Byzantine slumber'. Even a mature ecosystem needs small perturbations, just as we need challenges. The lesson of Gaian health is not simply to reach homeostasis and stability. Rather, such systems, and by extension architecture, might do well to be subject to intermittent probes, small shocks, less-than-lethal challenges.

In short, if Gaia is the model, we need an architecture of great organizational depth, exhibiting maximum diversity and robustness, but always unfinished and challenged in the parts. Modernists have not reached this conclusion but, as we will see in the next chapter, some of them are moving towards an architecture which acknowledges nature and the ecological predicament.

Frank Gehry, Chiat/Day Interior, *1991. Mixed use and genres make this a robust environment of complexity.*

XIX
HIGH-TECH SLIDES TO ORGANI-TECH

Every forty years or so Modern architects flirt with the concept and style of 'organicism'. Frank Lloyd Wright, of course, was deeply committed to his own version of Organic Architecture, so much so that he offered fifty-two definitions of it in one lecture and associated it with the free plan, free space, freedom from restraint and, in his romantic moments, free love. Rational organic architecture had exponents in the nineteenth century among engineers and Art Nouveau architects, and in the twentieth century it has been on the edge of Modernism with such architects as the German, Hugo Haring. But it has never occupied the center of the tradition, and even such a humanist as Alvar Aalto kept its expressive system as a minor element in his overall aesthetic. Curves, undulations and natural forms were mostly confined to ashtrays, door knobs and an occasional acoustic form, where they could be justified rationally and economically. The mind-set remained primarily deterministic.

So it has gone. High-Tech architecture, which developed within Modernism in the late 1960s, cast one eye at the organic metaphor of design, but only when it was structurally justified; otherwise remaining fully committed to the utilitarian and economic imperatives of modernity, which do not normally have a place

Richard Rogers and Renzo Piano, Pompidou Centre, *gerberettes, Paris 1971-77.*

for aesthetic concerns or our connection to nature. The Pompidou Center in Paris is typical in this respect. Designed by Richard Rogers and Renzo Piano in 1971, it is fundamentally a utilitarian packaging of warehouse space and a celebration of technological systems, except in one way: the human-like elbows, or *gerberettes*, which hold up the outside exoskeleton. These taper from the main columns to the outside 'hands' which in turn hold onto the thinner columns and cross-braces. Cast in steel in the shape of a tapering bone and joint, they are almost a perfect structural diagram of the forces within. Placed at dramatic points at the end of the building, they seemed to promise an opening of Modernism to nature and zöomorphic metaphor, a new appreciation of Antonio Gaudi's great expressive architecture of fifty years earlier. Alas, it was not to be. The High-Tech school, led by British architects, focused on other parts of the Pompidou: the mechanical services, anonymous shed-space, economical packaging and repetition.

By the mid 1980s this tradition became the dominant one of Modernism. The Hong Kong Bank and Lloyds' of London were its two establishment monuments, both Foster and Rogers were given knighthoods, and a host of further High-Tech architects were given Gold Medals at the Royal Institute of British Architects. They all confirmed its basic values.

However, even within Britain the approach varied widely, from the sober rationality of Michael Hopkins to the visionary ad hocism of Archigram, to the tough-minded realism of Cedric Price, to the engineering inventiveness of Ove Arup and Partners, to the poetic detailing of Nicholas Grimshaw. Although dominant, it was hardly a single approach. Other countries such as Germany and Japan gave it still other qualities, including the lightweight Silver Aesthetic. Almost all of this work, however brilliant in its own terms, suffers from the chronic maladies of Modernism: from the propensity to repeat good solutions *ad nauseum* – 'Monothematatis' – from reductivism, mechanism and functional determinism. Since I have already fumigated these diseases, I will confine my remarks to the positive emergent aspects of Modernism.

Now that ecology has become a mainstream concern, with big businesses and public bodies seeking long-term energy savings, and (because of robotic production and new materials) it is possible to build curved forms almost as cheaply and easily as straight ones, many architectural firms are adopting the slightly curved roof form. Arches, elliptical domes and s-curve solar collectors top many buildings in Britain and Europe. MacCormac Jamieson Prichard's award-winning Cable & Wireless Building is typical of the best, with its undulating waves of blue faience tiles rolling across the landscape in stately procession.

Even more committed to the curve as an *a priori* solution is the Spanish architect-engineer Santiago Calatrava who, as far as I know, has never managed to produce a building without several bends. His swooping bridges usually have slightly swelling curves that lean away from the center of the mass, thus setting up a dynamic tension with what they hold. They are lessons in counterthrust – what I would call frozen movement and although for the most part unmoving, they seem elastic and stretched.

Perhaps this is why his work is so popular and the subject of so many exhibitions: it has affinities with the tensed, moving body of an animal, and people naturally identify with that. Like the *gerberettes* at the Pompidou, some of his work, especially that influenced by Gaudi, is based on the structural shapes of bones, such as the nave design for the Cathedral of St John the Divine. Here we find not only the animal spine and rib-cage, but the tree, as implicit generators. While much of Calatrava's design looks muscle-bound at first, a bit too obvious and monumental – 'perilously close to kitsch . . . uncomfortably like the kind of place that would make Saddam Hussein feel at home', as Deyan Sudjic perhaps overstated the case[47] – it is actually inventive and subtle on second glance.

His Lyons train station for the airport connection seems to be just a spiky version of Saarinen's 'bird of flight' done for TWA at Kennedy Airport, New York, thirty years earlier; a symbol of flying turned into the logo for a whole building. In plan it is a bird, and from the two end elevations its wings of black and white metal seem to be flapping like a seagull trying to get airborn – the image in his mind. The metaphor is, however, tied to other ones – from the side a burrowing ant-eater and along the inside the more finely detailed filagree of a dragonfly's wing. A backbone spine of dazzling black and white chevrons skews the image another way, while its huge vaulting size immediately gives associations with dinosaurs. Almost every constructional member has some rationale, so there are also ways of reading the forms as utilitarian (although at £64 million the monument is overambitious in terms of the relatively few transients it serves).

One can quibble with the structural exhibitionism and wish there were still more frames of reference and metaphors, but this building – coming from within the tradition of Modernism – has something to remind that tradition about today. The repeated structural members have both *natural* metaphorical references and they *vary* slightly, just as one's own backbones differ. Monothematatis is robbed of some of its boredom.

It is true that all of the curves follow predictable developments – they graduate or diminish in a continuous manner and follow familiar shapes and crescendi. In this sense they are still clichés, and probably why so many of his structures are, at once, great popular successes and critical failures. Calatrava does bring structural metaphor back to architecture, he does use the natural curves of the body and has evolved a way of representing frozen movement – all positive contributions – but he has not gone the next step, as Gaudi did, of

ABOVE, OPPOSITE and OVERLEAF, LEFT: Santiago Calatrava, TGV Station, *Lyon-Satolas Airport, France, 1989-94. Natural metaphors – bird, anteater, bones, insect – return to structural design.*

mixing counter movements and using unfamiliar shapes. As we will see, the High-Tech English architect Nicholas Grimshaw has partly achieved this.

Renzo Piano has designed perhaps the largest metaphorical building in the world: the Kansai airport terminal in Osaka Bay, Japan. From the air it is a long, low silver glider with a wingspan of one mile and a head that burrows under its wings (a sleeping bird). Piano, the co-designer with Richard Rogers of the Pompidou Center, keeps a commitment to technical expressionism in the steel roof and white steel trusses – the skin and bones of this undulating glider. But what is new is the organic curves of the giant roof. These, like Calatravian curves, spring from bone-like triangular struts, and the interior shows again the spine-like backbones. As we walk through the airport we could be inside a natural history museum of stacked, parallel, dinosaur ribs. Exhilarating but slightly clinical.

It is an impressive space of swooping curves made more streamlined by the white canopies which zoom overhead, smoothing the way for the flow of air-conditioning. The air movement, seismic stresses and external envelope requirements determined the shape of the overall curve. Piano remains, in this sense, a deterministic functionalist. Unfortunately this commitment also means that the curves themselves are softened, predictable and, worst of all, bent down just where they should be opened up: in the direction of movement, towards the airplanes. It is true the mile-long glazed concourse allows some release in this direction, but hardly enough for the gesture itself.

This is undoubtedly one of the great megastructures of the late twentieth century, and the most ambitious airport since Saarinen's Dulles in the mid 60s. The artificial island on which it is built cost $14 billion to construct, and the building had to be jacked up and down as the island sank, making it one of the engineering wonders of the world. Given this high visibility, and Piano's undoubted skill, it is a shame the structure has some drawbacks. Let me repeat this boring point until it is accepted by Modernists (which, alas, is unlikely): this is Monothematatis on a positively colossal scale. The repetition of the roof unit of construction is so unvarying – a mile of the same unit! – that even Andy Warhol would go to sleep.

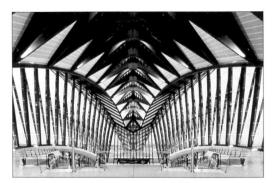 

ABOVE RIGHT AND OPPOSITE: R Piano, Kansai International Airport Terminal, *Japan.*

What can be said in its defence? Well, it is sublime like the desert, or a very smooth ocean, and the sublime is a potentially cosmic experience. Whether a utilitarian airport, without further dramatization and a symbolic programme underscoring transcendent meaning, can sustain this idea is partly a matter of taste. Some like to find their cosmic experience in the abstract and untouched – the Minimalist shapes of Carl Andre — and they may be moved by the extreme repetition. But most people would demand something more articulated, referential and complex.

In the circulation through the building, Piano has achieved some of this complexity by creating a sequence of space which changes between a grand 'canyon' just after the entrance, several layers of sandwich space, the undulating curve and the long concourse. There is also his continuing commitment to ecological concerns, evident in the tree-planting program (using indigenous Japanese species) which extends down the canyon and around the airport. As in his office in Genoa, and many public buildings, he tries to interpenetrate low-scaled architecture with nature. Much of this work could be called 'green architecture' of the disappearing variety: an unassertive, sensible, well-scaled and pleasant environment of energy-efficient building, rather than an architectural statement or visual investigation. This attitude makes Piano the greenest of the Modernists. Furthermore, he may be beginning to see the point of the sciences of complexity, and appears to be asking for a new architecture arising from them:

> There is a natural discipline that comes from life. And, once you accept that, you realize that architecture today must be reinvented. The revolution in science has to be interpreted in terms of social life. You have new technologies, new materials, new processes, and new aesthetics, and these elements that have been changing so drastically in the last fifty years make it necessary to invent a new architecture. I think in twenty years' time we will be much closer to craftsmanship – craftsmanship by computer. It is really a turning point in the art of making.[48]

 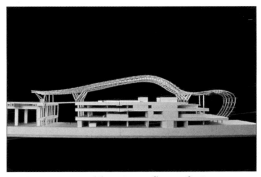

Renzo Piano, Kansai International Airport. *Seismic stress and laminar flow of air.*

Such words reveal a partial understanding of the new paradigm, even if in the end it is filtered through the Modernist commitment to 'new technologies, new materials, new processes' – that is: 'make it new' more than 'reconsider the fundamentals'. Piano is not about to embrace a full cosmogenic design, but he fully appreciates the shift possible with computer design and the new life sciences. That is some change.

His former partner, now Sir Richard Rogers, also speaks for a change in paradigm, and has said to me 'there has been a big shift in our work'.[49] We were talking about ecology and the recent turn towards curved forms and organic shapes called 'technorganic' by the English critic John Welsh.[50] My counter argument to both Welsh and Rogers was that this shift was more a slide, and it was towards 'organi-tech' not the reverse. Why? Because technology and the utilitarian concerns are still predominate over nature and the organic. There has been a slide in emphasis but still the biomorphic element is very much tertiary and, indeed, ecology is secondary. In primary place is still repetition, the shed, utility and, yes, the Machine Aesthetic – even if it is less aggressive than at the Pompidou Center.

Nonetheless, Rogers' architecture has changed, particularly now that it is being generated by ecological concerns. This was first evident around 1990 when he produced a scheme for a tower in Tokyo with an aerofoil shape – to speed up the movement of wind around the building and thus ventilate it and lower energy consumption. A proposal for an Inland Revenue building resulted in a cross-section which naturally ventilates a structure. By creating a hot air bubble at the top of an atrium, between roof and sun shades, and by pushing this bubble to the edge of the atrium, he naturally draws cooler air through the bottom floors. This, the stack effect, then pulls fresh air through, an idea which he used on the Daimler-Benz offices in Berlin.

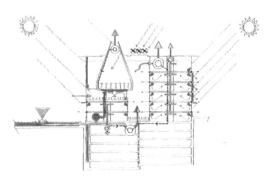

Richard Rogers Partnership, Magistrates Courts, extension, Bordeaux, 1993- . Seven courts, pods creating a stack effect with skylights, sit in a glazed grid; the temperature is made cooler in summer or hotter in winter by using the adjacent pool as a moderating system.

Rogers has combined the stack effect with the now fashionable blob-shape in several schemes under construction, such as the Magistrates Courts in Bordeaux. In the historic part of the old city there are seven identical 'mushrooms' – again High-Tech, remorseless repetition – suspended inside a thinner structure of arches, columns and glass walls. The solution has a radical logic to it. Each court room looks through the glass wall to the square and water. Private offices behind, public spaces expressed clearly in front, for the *res publica*. Energy efficiency is provided by an ingenious use of the water gardens, piping in its liquid to cool in the summer and heat in the winter. The cone-blobs, which are cut on the north-angle to block out the strong southern sun, also create a stack effect with their pinched shape. Cooling, in effect, generates the mushroom that looks like a small power station, or the chapel design Le Corbusier produced for Firminy, France just before his death in 1965.

With this scheme Rogers signals he is right at the cusp of biomorphic design: will he, like Gehry and others, drop his commitment to the technological imperative and embrace a more fluid architecture? There are possibilities here even within a High-Tech approach, as Jan Kaplicky and Amanda Levete of Future Systems have shown with their egg-shaped schemes for offices. These ovoid-blobs also make use of the stack effect and aerofoil shape to accelerate wind. A biomorphic turn is possible, but it is unlikely, given the obligation of High-Tech architects to express the regularity and rationality of structure.

Much more likely is the combination seen in Rogers' recent competition winner for the South Bank culture center in London. Here we find the cross between waves and a repetitive roof structure, actually a cone of eight undulations and a net of canopies. The combination is both a biomorphic 'eye' and technological grid of standardized elements – the typical hybrid of 'organi-tech', with equal emphasis on both sides of the duality. On one level it is a breathtaking

 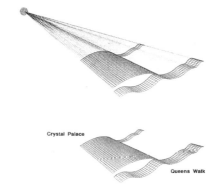

Richard Rogers Partnership, South Bank Transformation, *Competition Winner, London, 1994. Waves of eight unseen cones generate a petal effect roof which undulates over existing structures and moderates the temperature.*

simplification of a complex site. A glass and opaque canopy (blocking out south light) covers several concrete buildings, just as Buckminster Fuller wanted to cover much of New York City with a glass dome.

But, thankfully, here there is a brilliant sideways-thought. This is not a univalent dome, a megalomaniacal, single gesture dominating a whole area, as was Fuller's proposal. Rather, as the cone-drawing shows, it is articulated in eight ups and downs; self-similar forms which focus perspectively further south of the site, several blocks away. These cone-sections were generated by two bridges that frame the site at an angle. If you continue their lines they meet as the apex of a big cone, which is then sliced into smaller sections. Generating undulating lines from this point allows the roof structure to rise over most of the concrete buildings where it needs to, and split into a river-front covered walk elsewhere.

The whole 'crystal palace', if built, has an interesting rationale: in a place where rain, wind and cold have discouraged people from going to concerts and art galleries, this new roof structure will transport the culture centre to the climate of Bordeaux. It may rain on the outside, but the mean temperature will be southern France on the inside; no small matter in a country where it is drizzly and grey half the year. One will have to await further design to see if enough variation and movement are brought into the scheme and its details, but at this stage it seems to be an important breakthrough for Rogers – the ability to design outside the model of technical and utilitarian expression with an entirely 'other' idea.

That one can get to unlikely models such as 'waves' and 'cones' from purely rational considerations is the obvious riposte, and I can hear the functionalists making it. No doubt it is important for them to think so, for how else are they to persuade the client that their leap of imagination – or *non sequitur* – must be built. Technological determinism is the occupational hazard of the High-Tech architect: at a certain stage he must believe that design just happens automatically as a consequence of an initial decision. This explains why so much of the work is repetitive, the fatalistic recurrence of a structural bay and detail.

Nicholas Grimshaw, younger than the first generation of Foster, Piano, Rogers and Hopkins, started to push repetitive, structural design in a more poetic direction with his newspaper plant in Plymouth, finished in 1992. This has the overall shape of a doubly-curved ship, with walls of glass curving convex in plan and concave in elevation. Much more challenging, because it mixes several structural shapes in opposition and on a curve, is his Waterloo terminal for the Channel Tunnel. Here we find, at least on the inside with its shimmering glass, a real image of a twisting, snakelike architecture, close to nature. On one reading the snake was a pure result of fatalistic, Darwinian design: the tracks curve and each set gets closer to the adjacent one as they leave the station – so the roof must curve and taper. Given the initial decision by Grimshaw, that it be glazed on its west side and meet the low canopy on the east, it deterministically became a three-pinned arch with a glass curve set against an asymmetrical truss.

So far so fatalistic. The next necessity was to design the glass panes and their stabilizing glass fins – all 1,728 of them, all *slightly different* – so they could keep out the rain and move up and down when a train rumbled through. A computer calculated these snake-scales exactly – self-similar forms if ever. The exterior of this sinuous worm may be somewhat confused, with its blue bones fighting the transparent skin, but the interior is a recognized masterpiece of 'organi-tech', the first building which can be compared to Gaudian architecture without apology. It uses structure as a changing, oppositional set of systems. They fly about in a ballet of give and take, the very image of living form.

Grimshaw himself appreciates the oblique view of the rippling glass skin as 'paddy fields'. Other British critics committed to High-Tech also seem poised to recognize the building as a challenge to previous assumptions about repetition, organicism, metaphor and the public realm. It is an obligation of the architect to be accessible, relate to nature and follow the changing edge of science and technology. Here Grimshaw does it. Might the other Modernists follow suit – will the slide become a flow?

ABOVE AND OVERLEAF: Nicholas Grimshaw and Partners, Waterloo Channel Tunnel Terminal, *London, 1990-1993. Sheets of glass move up and down independently as trains decelerate and the whole station groans under the braking weight. The 3-pinned curving snake results from technical considerations, which are eased in a biomorphic direction.*

PART THREE

COSMOGENIC ARCHITECTURE

Frank Gehry, Guggenheim Museum, *Bilbao, Spain, 1992-97. An architecture of twists, waves, undulations, smooth continuity and punctuation.*

XX

THE SURPRISING UNIVERSE AND COSMIC ARCHITECTURE

If architecture must be oriented to nature and culture, then it also must have a larger orientation: the universe as a whole. Architecture has always had some cosmic dimension in traditional cultures. In India, Egypt, Greece, Japan, and in the West throughout the Renaissance, architects inscribed the cosmos in their buildings, oriented their structures to the propitious points of the universe and represented it in the details. Today architecture must also do these things, as well as go beyond this to our contemporary view; that is, cosmogenesis.

Even the Modern Movement, for a short period after the First World War, sought to ground its buildings in the science of the day. A group of Expressionists produced an abundance of creative responses to the cosmos as revealed in mystical, religious, and scientific writings – all three. In his magazine *Fruhlicht* ('Early Light') and in his building projects of the early 1920s, Bruno Taut explored the metaphysics of light as revealed by medieval mystics and contemporary research into crystals. A crystalline repetition of glass elements with multiple facets facing different directions, and light bursting through like an explosion of sunlight, became the visual metaphor for his metaphysics. Others, such as Hermann Finsterlin and Rudolph Steiner, followed a more anthropomorphic direction and produced an undulating architecture with sexual and viscous metaphors.

FROM LEFT TO RIGHT: WA Hablik, Cycle of Buildings – Cubes (Calcareous Spar)*, 1921. A crystalline architecture was proposed for a short period before the Machine Age ground it down; E Mendelsohn,* Einstein Tower, *Potsdam, Germany 1917-21. Zöomorphic expression – the warping of spacetime by matter; V Tatlin,* Monument to the Third International, *1919-20. Four Platonic volumes rotate daily, weekly, monthly, yearly, hold main organs of World government, while the spiral movement up and down relates to the punctuated growth of the cosmos.*

Erich Mendelsohn even managed to work on a commission that combined the new cosmology and the new Expressionism. His Einstein Tower in Potsdam, 1917-21, is less tower than grasping animal. It lies on the ground and reaches forward with its arms to embrace the astronomers and welcome them up to its 'head', the dome holding the coelostat and instruments which were to measure Einstein's General Theory of Relativity. Unfortunately, some technical details were not worked out, and the Theory was checked first elsewhere. But, as a visual metaphor of Einstein's Theory, the tower worked as Mendelsohn planned, showing, by analogy with straight lines turning into continuous curves that never stop, that matter could turn continuously into energy, and vice-versa.

A few other Modernists designed exemplary buildings that sought to express the poetic equivalent of cosmology. Vladimir Tatlin's Monument to the Third International is easily the most interesting of these projects combining, as it does in its rotations and primary forms, the dialectical movement of history *and* the cosmos. Terragni's work on the Danteum and Le Corbusier's work at Chandigarh are more private and less scientific in their treatment of cosmic themes, portending the widening gap between the two cultures which has continued to expand until recently.

Today, however, the time is propitious for a rapprôchement between the arts and cosmology. This is due, as much as anything, to the confluence of ideas within the various sciences, to the way Complexity Theory, Chaos Theory, Quantum Theory and Cosmology give congruent pictures of the universe. It is true that Relativity and Quantum Theories have yet to be reconciled, but anticipations of a resolution have been proposed in the idea of Superstrings and the 'Theory of Everything'. The last appellation shows just how hubristic and dotty recent science has become, since this cannibalistic theory does not even cover much more than fundamental forces and particles; does not even begin to deal with the emergent things that really interest us.

At the same time contemporary science has become grand and ambitious, universal and cross-disciplinary. Never has it been so speculative and creative, popular and engaging. We are living through the first real explosion of scientific culture into the mass media, a popularity which dwarfs that of the eighteenth century. With ten or so best-selling scientific writers such as Stephen Hawking and Paul Davies, basic thinking on time, cosmology and purpose in the universe have become popular issues. The succession of new scientific theories begins to resemble a 'new dialogue with nature', as Ilya Prigogine calls it, an exciting discourse between hypothesis and refutation, and not the imperious discourse of certainty and fixed truth it has been in the past.

Some of this shift is due to the recent appreciation of time in the scientific paradigm: the notion that evolution is essential to all things, not peripheral; the idea that the universe is an unfinished process not an eternal thing. In the Newtonian universe the direction of time did not matter; equations worked just as well backwards as forwards, and scientists up to and including Einstein thought they were dealing with an unchanging set of laws. But, one after another, the Post-Modern sciences of complexity started to challenge this static picture of the universe. In the nineteenth century the new sciences of thermodynamics and ecology introduced directionality and holism into the equations. Then between 1900 and 1927 quantum and relativity theories overturned determinism. In the late 1940s general systems theory, plus a series of life sciences and computer sciences started to grow, and by the late 1970s the trickle had become a flood, yielding a new consistent paradigm. Continuing the Post-Modern perceptions of the cosmos, Chaos theory, fractals, neural nets and Gaia have arrived on the scene. All of this can be generally conceived as the sciences of complexity, or nonlinear dynamics, or self-organizing systems. They were understood, by their creators if not everyone, to be more pertinent than the old Modern sciences of simplicity – and to sublate or include them as limiting cases.

Fundamentally, we started to move into a universe of cosmogenesis instead of a static cosmos. I say 'started' advisedly since the new paradigm is not yet accepted by the whole scientific community. But I believe it will be by the next generation, because it is more fully explanatory than the old world view. As

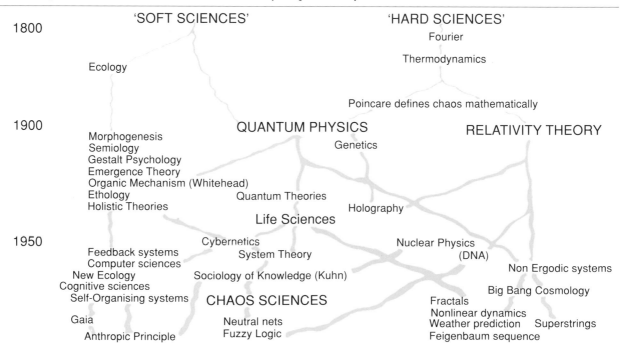

Post-Modern Sciences of Complexity *start with a trickle in the nineteenth century, deepen with Quantum and Relativity Theories in the early twentieth and then become an interconnected river delta by the end of the century, with nonlinear dynamics and chaos theory.*

scientists themselves explain: it takes a new crop of scientists to learn a new way of thinking, or, as they say more ironically, 'Physics advances death by death – where there's death, there's hope'.

What is the cosmogenic world view? It is the idea that the universe is a single, unfolding self-organizing event, something more like an animal than machine, something radically interconnected and creative, an entity that jumps suddenly to higher levels of organization and delights us as it does so.[51] Complexity Theory, the Gaia hypothesis, Chaos and Quantum theories all point in this direction. We know truths that have been revealed to no other generation, and they can give us great hope and strength.

Fundamentally, the new understanding of reality overturns the four great enslaving 'isms' of Modernity: determinism, mechanism, reductivism, and materialism. The new concepts which have replaced them are emergence, self-organization, evolution by punctuated equilbria, and cosmogenesis – creativity as basic in the universe.

They refute the nihilistic view, developed because of Modern determinism and materialism, that our place in the universe is accidental, tangential, absurd and discontinuous with the rest of nature. Rather they show, as Freeman Dyson put it: 'the universe must have known we were coming', or, in Paul Davies' words: 'that we are built into the laws of the universe in some fundamental ways'. Mind, consciousness, and sentient creatures with intelligence are not alien to, but *central* to the cosmogenic process.

Perhaps the biggest surprise is that we can talk of the origin and development of the universe, at least back to the first few seconds, and therefore derive a classical picture of where we stand. What does this standard model look like? One way of representing it is as an unfolding flower, or trumpet, or vase. Fifteen billion years ago, or at the beginning of time, there was a little ripple, or quantum fluctuation, or 'flaring forth' – or, as the popular Modern metaphor – originally intended to be derisive – would have it: 'Big Bang'. The metaphor, or representation, does matter, as Post-Modernists remind us, since as we construct these mental pictures they then construct us. Whichever image we pick, this 'event' then underwent extreme expansion, from the size of a quark to something a billion billion times bigger – the size of a grapefruit.

This period of rapid expansion, known as inflation, fine-tuned the forces and the subsequent expansion so that the universe could evolve successfully. If it had unfolded too fast, with too much force, it would have burst apart into pluriverses; if it had been too weak, the force of gravity would have squeezed it to death. The balance had to be perfect, or as close to perfect as you can think: 'The kinetic energy and the gravitational energy of the universe had to be initially equal[52] to one part in 10^{59}'. Imagine that accurate an initial setting – to

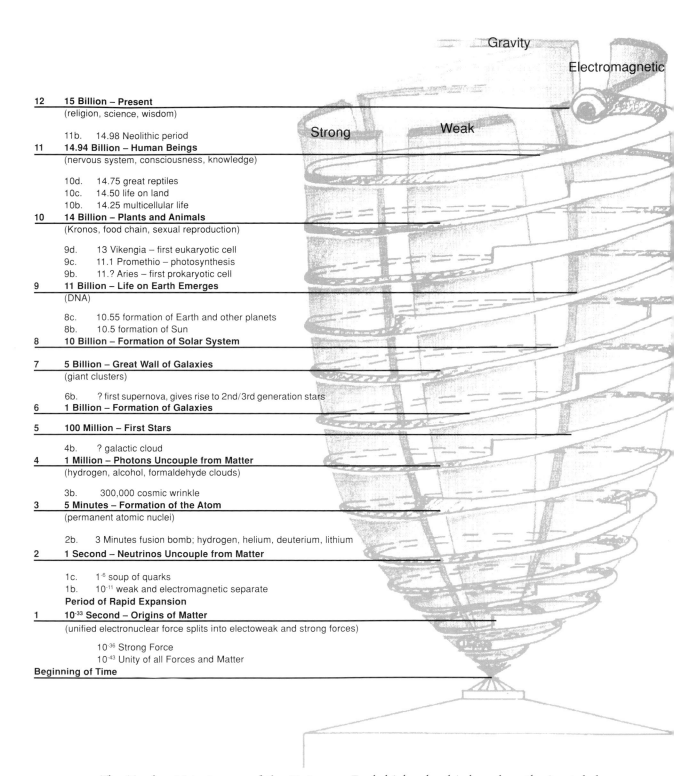

12	**15 Billion – Present**		
	(religion, science, wisdom)		
	11b. 14.98 Neolithic period		
11	**14.94 Billion – Human Beings**		
	(nervous system, consciousness, knowledge)		

Labels on figure: Gravity, Electromagnetic, Strong, Weak

12   **15 Billion – Present**
     (religion, science, wisdom)

     11b.   14.98 Neolithic period
11   **14.94 Billion – Human Beings**
     (nervous system, consciousness, knowledge)

     10d.   14.75 great reptiles
     10c.   14.50 life on land
     10b.   14.25 multicellular life
10   **14 Billion – Plants and Animals**
     (Kronos, food chain, sexual reproduction)

     9d.   13 Vikengia – first eukaryotic cell
     9c.   11.1 Promethio – photosynthesis
     9b.   11.? Aries – first prokaryotic cell
9   **11 Billion – Life on Earth Emerges**
     (DNA)

     8c.   10.55 formation of Earth and other planets
     8b.   10.5 formation of Sun
8   **10 Billion – Formation of Solar System**

7   **5 Billion – Great Wall of Galaxies**
     (giant clusters)

     6b.   ? first supernova, gives rise to 2nd/3rd generation stars
6   **1 Billion – Formation of Galaxies**

5   **100 Million – First Stars**

     4b.   ? galactic cloud
4   **1 Million – Photons Uncouple from Matter**
     (hydrogen, alcohol, formaldehyde clouds)

     3b.   300,000 cosmic wrinkle
3   **5 Minutes – Formation of the Atom**
     (permanent atomic nuclei)

     2b.   3 Minutes fusion bomb; hydrogen, helium, deuterium, lithium
2   **1 Second – Neutrinos Uncouple from Matter**

     1c. 1^{-6} soup of quarks
     1b. 10^{-11} weak and electromagnetic separate
     Period of Rapid Expansion
1   **10^{-33} Second – Origins of Matter**
     (unified electronuclear force splits into electoweak and strong forces)

       10^{-36} Strong Force
       10^{-43} Unity of all Forces and Matter
Beginning of Time

The Twelve Main Jumps of the Universe. *Each higher level is based on the jump below, raising the question of whether we could have got here sooner, in a different way, and how far we are built into the laws that have generated the process. Did the universe know we were coming? The eye of consciousness reflects back on the universe.*

within one-over-one followed by fifty-nine zeroes – and you are as close to a miracle of fine-tuning as you will get. There is no other event as unlikely except the creation itself.

After this quick expansion, still at a trillionth of a second, the electronuclear force (the basic unity of the universe) split into Gravity, the Electroweak and Strong forces, giving us three of the basic four forces that rule the physical world. Soon thereafter, at 10^{-11} of a second, the Weak nuclear force emerged, and in this form the basic laws of electricity, magnetism and nuclear explosions have remained the same ever since. Before this, before the forces 'froze out' of an expanding, cooling universe, there was just one unified force. So basic laws *do* evolve, even if rarely and more slowly than, say, social and economic laws.

I do not intend to continue explaining the next fifteen billion years in a similar vein, but I should mention the dramatic jumps in organization because they constitute the narrative of the continuous, unfolding event we call cosmogenesis. If everything were a soup of quarks for the first second, then the most dramatic event was the emergence of matter from this plasma field of energy. 'Let there be light', and only light, for the first seconds, and let there be matter and energy for the next eleven billion years – when they were joined by life. The intervening time saw the sudden creation of atoms, photons, stars, galaxies, walls of galaxies and the solar system. Each entity was a surprise, and each one presupposed the one before.

Thus it is necessary that stars collapse and explode as supernovae before heavier elements, and life, are possible. Thus it is necessary that a certain amount of time passes, and many other creations exist, before the universe can produce a sentient creature. There is sequence and direction in this, as long as it is qualified as a predisposition and not predetermination. The universe seemingly had to produce organisms like us, if not exactly us, after fourteen billion years. Again, the story of the evolution of life from the first prokaryotic cells to the reptiles and birds and hominids is now canonic and well known. There are disputes about the exact sequence, but the general jumps in organization are not doubted.

The runaway creation of oxygen by photosynthesis – to make the explosive cocktail which runs Gaia; the invention of sex – to multiply genetic diversity and make life more enjoyable (and problematic); the invention of language – to make thought more powerful and shared; the invention of mind, the most complex thing in the universe – to reflect back on, intervene in, and celebrate the cosmogenesis; the emergence of culture – to feed back on the previous levels, amplify creativity and make it all worth while, a virtuous rather than vicious circle. Each of these creations was a sudden, surprising jump in organizational depth, an increase in complexity, a new era in cosmic history, and each one also had some tragic consequences .

The general rule is that the more creative the universe the more the potential for benevolence and for suffering. Catastrophe, chaos, sudden mass-extinctions are just as deep and essential to the account as the growing organization and beauty. The view of the cosmic process is decidedly mixed. It reveals that we emerged because of an asteroid that hit the planet near the Gulf of Mexico sixty-five million years ago and wiped out the dinosaurs. One can be optimistic about the overall process, and pessimistic about the details – 'tragic optimism'.

Such a contradictory attitude, such a paradox mixing opposing mental states, is a realistic mind-set for the contrary evidence. And, returning to architecture for a moment, a mixed representation of this cosmic reality is warranted, a building approach that expresses the order that emerges from chaos as well as the entropy which results as a consequence.

A basic narrative of the cosmos has been written by Brian Swimme and Thomas Berry as *The Universe Story* (1992). They recount this history as a single, unfolding narrative with many subplots. No previous age could incorporate cosmogenesis and history into such a grand metanarrative; the information and theories simply did not exist before the 1960s. One can criticize Berry and Swimme's account, including its univocal tone, but I think the two authors are basically right to say that such a story constitutes a meta-religion for all cultures, whether they are theist, aethiest, ancient, native, or modern. No one can escape the implications of this story.

As we know from psychologists, narratives shape, sustain, and direct the individual personality. The 'self' develops through learning an enormous number of stories and fitting them into a coherent metanarrative. With the challenge to conventional religious and materialist stories, conflict and disorientation have necessarily increased. Given the resultant confusion, one can see all the more how the new cosmic metanarrative could provide a spiritual and cultural grounding.

Yet this idea is bound to be resisted, partly because we have had so many false unifications of science, religion and culture since the Enlightenment; that is, since they became specialized and went their separate ways. Also, it is a matter of politics and temperament. Many will prefer a fragmented 'war of language games', as do most Deconstructionists, because they feel a unified culture is inherently totalitarian for individuals. Nevertheless, I believe there are compelling arguments for regarding the new emergent story of cosmogenesis as a common narrative with spiritual implications.

Responsibility For Metaphor
Translating this story into architecture presents some difficulties. How do we interpret and depict it? Indeed, while a lot of the facts and a narrative have been agreed, they are underinterpreted by theologians and philosophers. In addition,

there are different models which lend themselves as appropriate interpretations, but none is completely adequate. For instance, the same set of evidence I have set out above as a flower or vase can also be interpreted as a circle of trumpets or a rotating spiral. Each model may depict inflation and the jumps in history, but in entirely different ways.

The choice of a model or interpretive metaphor has to be made also because the evidence is, in some sense, underdetermined. Perhaps in certain cases we need beauty to make the universe itself choose one route rather than another; certainly aesthetics plays a big role in the way scientists choose between competing hypotheses. Surprisingly, many architects today give up aesthetic responsibility and hide behind cost, function, planning requirements or some other alibi. Yet if the lesson of recent cosmology is that the environment is not determined, then architecture is even less so; architects have the freedom to choose style, metaphor and form language. Indeed, they have the obligation to do so – virtually their most open choice.

Concerning the model of the universe, something can be said for adopting the Big Bang metaphor if one likes video-nasties, and one's idea of power is the Pentagon. But the idea of the universe as a big explosion does not help us see the more subtle, unfolding and beautiful aspects. There is a direct architectural

Charles Jencks, Joanna Migdal, Universe Model, Mark II, *1994 (work in progress). Cosmogenesis represented as a spiral of growth generates a globe which unfolds in distinct jumps. The model is an alternative to that on page 126.*

expression of these choices. During the First World War and under the Fascists, the Futurists developed an extensive 'aesthetics of war', which celebrated, in one of its exponents' ringing words, 'gas masks, terrifying megaphones, flame throwers and small tanks'. Fillipo Tomaso Marinetti proclaimed in a 1930s Futurist Manifesto: 'War is beautiful because it creates a new architecture, like that of the big tanks, the geometrical formation flights, the smoke spirals from burning villages . . . ' (sic)

The popularity of Clint Eastwood, *Robocop*, and Operation Desert Storm shows that this aesthetics of war is not entirely exhausted. The architectural fashion for slashes, zaps and deconstructive collisions dominates the schools. Heavy metal and S&M-High-Tech create the major trend of 'Post-Holocaust Design'. Like the arms trade, Big Bang thinking is very much alive.

So, choose another aesthetic of life, of undulating movement, of surprising humour, of catastrophic folds and delightful waves, of billowing crystals and fractured planes, of layered glass and spiralling growth. Quantum physics is behind it, pushing, while the continuously unfolding cosmos is ahead, luring one on; not designing like an architect, but gestating and giving birth, like a fecund animal.

One might press on in this vein, especially when confronted with the Neo-Warfare Style so popular in Post-Bosnia culture, but the point is made: there is freedom, there is choice, in a predispositionist universe. As Virgil said: 'We make our destinies through the gods we choose'.

Cosmic Architecture

Let us look quickly at the variety of cosmic architecture and compare it to the related and more recently developed 'cosmogenic architecture' – both are importantly diverse and alternatives to mainstream, neutral Modernism.

Japanese designers are at one of the forefronts of thinking on cosmic architecture, perhaps because of their traditions of Zen Buddhism, Neo-Confucianism and Shintoism. These belief-systems are often more open to the metaphysics of contemporary science than those in the West, where there is a protracted war between Christianity and Modern science.

Arata Isozaki, developing the static type of cosmic architecture, has based it on a wry monumentalism that poses humorous questions. His first essay, the Fujimi Country Club (1972), is a giant concrete barrel vault in the shape of a question-mark, posing the question that is on everyone's mind today (since the overbuilding of country clubs burst with the economic bubble in 1991): 'Why *do* the Japanese play golf?' The question, which may seem trivial, actually goes to the heart of Japanese identity and is tantamount to asking: 'Why do they copy Western technology so well; why are they taking over the world economy?'

At the Tsukuba Civic Center (1983), Isozaki, designing in multiple, Western codes (ten different styles), further developed his notion that Japanese identity was based on mimicking endless texts outside the center of local culture – a superabundant eclecticism – and a consequent notion that what is really distinctively Japanese is the void at the center. Thus the whole complex focuses on a fountain and waterfall which drains towards Mother Earth, a black hole which is meant to symbolize the 'presence of the absence' at the heart of society; the fact that everyone in Japan feels the Emperor's presence in the center of Tokyo, but no one can see him.

There is something very elusive and ambiguous in Isozaki's approach that is hard for a Westerner to understand. I have known 'Iso' for twenty years and confess that he continues to surprise and disturb me, especially in his recent 'black period', which seems preoccupied with death. But perhaps this is one of his strong points – to produce buildings that disturb categories of perception, to fall between pigeonholes. His Disney Headquarters Building in Orlando, Florida, for Disney executives and employees, is characteristic of this ambiguity. On one level, especially on the exterior, it is a brash Pop collage of Mickey Mouse ears and Rationalist architecture, of dayglo red, pinks, and greens – an appropriately manic expression of 'Have A Nice Day' (or you will be fired). On the inside, the central cylinder is a calm, even frightening, cosmic space, with big stones as a floor and a circle open to the sky above. The cone is sliced in sections by the violent opposition of Florida sunlight and deep shadow. Thus a walk-though sundial, time's image of creation and destruction, occupies the heart: the sub-

 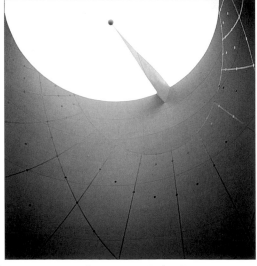

PREVIOUS PAGE AND ABOVE: Arata Isozaki, Disney Headquarters, *Lake Buena Vista, Florida, 1989-91. A Pop-collage on the exterior, with Mickey Mouse entrance and vibrating colours contrasts sharply with the cosmic dome open to the sky – sundial above a Japanese stone garden.*

lime in the banal, the sacred in the middle of the Empire of Trivial Pursuits. Here is the counterpart of recent evolution theory: punctuated equilibria, the universe as simultaneously horrific and harmonic.

For more than twenty years Monta Mozuna has been developing a cosmic architecture based on many historical systems: Shintoism and Buddhism as one might guess, but also Pythagoreanism, Chinese Yin and Yang symbols, Inca myths, Christian theology, and Carl Jung's archetypes. It sounds syncretic and whimsical, but it is not. A deep truth underlies the idea that no one metaphysical system is entirely adequate, that all of them have illuminated some cosmic truths and, collectively, that they show both the cosmic propensity for variety – its most profound pattern – and mixing.

Of course, all religions and scientific disciplines jealously guard the purity of their systems, and routinely excommunicate eclectics and synthesizers, but nature knows few such purists and their separated university departments. For the most part, the world is as radically mixed as the new science of Fuzzy Logic claims: most questions have a 'more or less' answer, very few an absolute 'right and wrong' solution. Hence the omnipresence of qualifier-words in common speech, the 'sort-ofs' and 'kind-ofs' that pepper conversations; hence NASA runs its docking spacecraft on Fuzzy Logic computer chips (they are less abrupt than either-or binary chips); hence most architecture is approximate and impure – Egyptian, Christian, Modernist, technological, vernacular, and other. Impure, on this reading, is kind-of profound because it is the prevalent situation of life. Monta Mozuna makes such hybridization a compositional method.

Kiko Monta Mozuna, Kushiro City Museum, *1982-4. Abstract representation of embracing wings on the exterior, and DNA, past, present and future on the inside.*

Mozuna's Kushiro City Museum (1982-4) facade presents the abstraction of two winged birds – one being the ancient symbol of the city. The outstretched wings, represented as superimposed tiers, embrace visitors as they approach the center of the building, which is a 'cosmic egg' and, on the inside, a dome represent the heavens. The three levels of organization hold the past (excavations), present (industry), and future (cranes against the sky), all of which are connected by a double-helical staircase symbolizing DNA, the strands of life.

Such monumental Post-Modern Classicism recalls the late period of Le Corbusier and Louis Kahn's work, also motivated by an attempt to ground us with a grand cosmic vision of land, sky, nature and pure form: the archetypes represented with Platonic certainty. Charles Correa's recent architecture in India continues this heroic tradition, but brings it into the late twentieth century by incorporating such things as black holes, fractals, and the plenum vacuum (the mystery at the heart of things; how something comes from 'nothing'). He has just completed five cosmic projects, the most relevant being an actual science center, the Inter-University Center for Astronomy and Astrophysics in Pune, India. Here we find, in his own words:

> . . . our own twentieth-century understanding of the the expanding universe in which scientists believe we dwell. Thus one arrives between black walls (local black basalt, surmounted by even blacker kuddapah stone, capped by glossy black polished granite, reflecting sky and clouds). Black on black on black – the infinity of outer space. The whole complex is arranged around a central kund (that ancient archetype for the cosmos) – but one which is expanding (exploding!) into peripheral systems of space. [53]

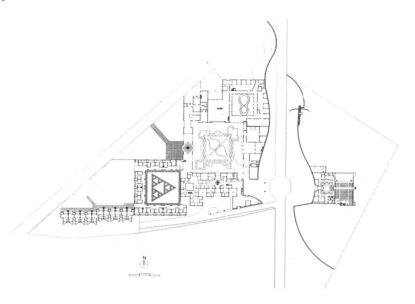

Charles Correa, Inter-University Center of Astronomy and Astrophysics, *Pune, India, 1990-93. Conceived as a model of the cosmos, the black stone entrance and center garden signify, respectively, the infinity of outer space and jets of energy emerging from a Black Hole. Other figures represent the ordered growth within chaos.*

The plan reveals the fractal pattern known as Serpenski's Gasket in one court-yard; the figure eight and infinity (Roche Lobes) in another, and a Black Hole in the center courtyard with energy being ejected on the diagonal. The specificity here is exemplary – Correa is trying in all this work to find appropriate scientific ideograms, diagrams and forms that can translate into architecture. It is not an easy task, as I can vouch, because many of the most important insights in current science are invisible. They are more easily represented by equations, words, and waving arms, than by big heavy things that sit on the ground getting wet!

Here we touch an essential problem: how is the permanent art of architecture to represent the changing, sometimes ephemeral, nature of reality? Itsuko Hasegawa has discovered one way, with her steely-grey aesthetic of undulating panels. For instance, her ST House in Tokyo consists of a series of perforated aluminium panels cut out in the shape of clouds and sine-curves. These wave-forms signify connections with nature, what she calls a second-nature that is built. The metallic forms are also particularly sensitive to changes in weather and light, reflecting them as a chameleon mirrors its environment. In addition, when perforated panels are layered, as in her Nagoya Expo Pavilion, the inter-ference patterns represent quantum physical phenomena quite literally. She has not, as yet, developed her architecture into a systematic representation of the cosmos, as has Monta Mozuna, but she is now actively engaged in exploring the new sciences of fractals, Fuzzy Logic, and chaos, all popular in Japan.

Nagoya Expo Pavilion, 1992. Wave forms and interference patterns reflect the changing dynamics of the quantum world; Itsuko Hasegawa, ST House, Tokyo, 1991.

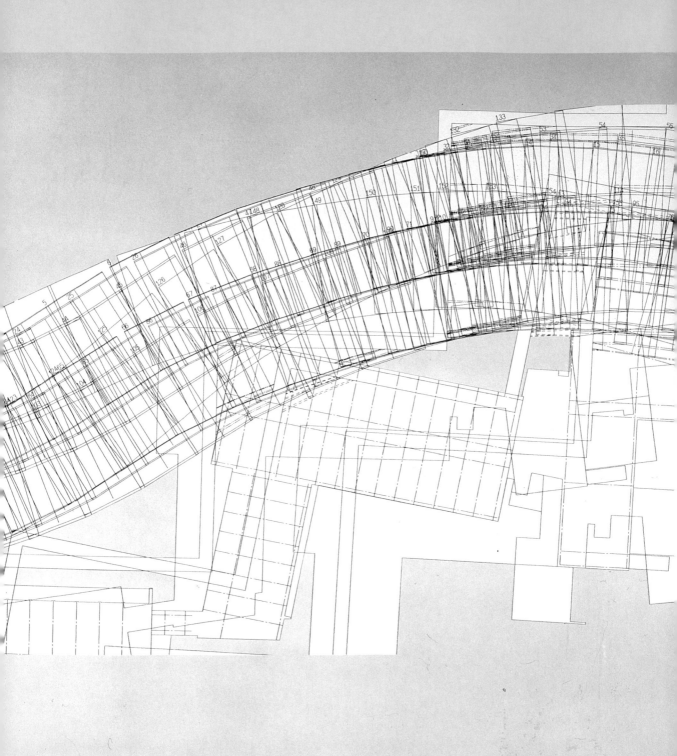

XXI

COSMOGENIC ARCHITECTURE

No one has looked to the lessons of emerging sciences more strenuously than Peter Eisenman. Since his early work in 'cardboard architecture' in the late 1960s, based loosely on the theories of Noam Chomsky and his concept of 'deep structure', Eisenman has picked up one *nuova scienta* after another, using devices drawn from fractals (self-similarity, scaling, superposition), from DNA research (his Bio-Centrum project), from Catastrophe Theory (the fold), from rhetoric (catechresis), from Boolean algebra (the hypercube), and from psychoanalysis (too many theories to remember). There is deep humour in all of this, Eisenman appears to take his borrowings from science only half-seriously, as if to say, in answer to the Modernists: scientific truths are a pretext for architecture, not the justification itself.

Theory for Eisenman is like a machine which automatically produces art when it is followed through systematically. The beauty of his work is that it is idea-led and thus, as one interprets it, there is always the transformation of certain concepts that provide consistency and drama. Secondly, the use of his science brings back a kind of Ruskinian 'savageness', a raw relation to truth outside the human condition. In an era when opinion and anthropocentricism dominate culture, this returns us to a non-human standard for architecture that used to be the preserve of religions. Today, when so much organized worship has become a branch of the comfort industry, the role of science is to discover this 'otherness', preserving a tradition in which it can be respected.

Eisenman's shift to the nonlinear sciences and a new urbanism began in 1987 and, as we have seen with his Rebstock Housing in Frankfurt, makes extensive use of the fold. His Cincinnati School of Art, Architecture and Planning intro-

Peter Eisenman, Department of Art, Architecture and Planning, University of Cincinnati, *1992-95. A key project mediating between the waves of landscape and the zig-zags of a pre-existing building. Surprisingly, waves of rectangles and squares oscillate between these two opposite systems on a small scale, thus beautifully smearing out the opposition between the grown and the made.*

duces the wave form as a transformation of the zig-zag rectangles of the existing school to which it is added. The space between the two is then a fragmented mixture, as if the rectangular and undulating waves washed up and back against each other, leaving traces. As Sanford Kwinter has shown, there is something of a strange attractor in the overall curved wave, as if it is oscillating about its center.[54] These oscillations and the stepped tilts of the small rectangles break up the volumes into a series of staccato staggers, which make the inert form shimmer.

This kind of architecture is more fluid and supple than the more familiar right-angled forms, or even those it is constructed from and adjacent to: the old building. Conceptually it is made from 'between forms'; forms that are both curves and straight lines, depending on the scale, and it begins to approximate a moving architecture, like Hasegawa's waves. In this sense it represents a cosmogenic process of continual unfolding, an emergence between the habitual categories which generate its existence. Whether it will be successful or inert, in the end, will remain in question until completion, sometime in late 1995.

In his Columbus Convention Center Eisenman takes this undulating wave, now a 'worm' or vermiform shape, and simplifies it because of the site and program. The vermiform shape comes from the lines generated by railroad tracks and freeways near the site and is an attempt to make an American architecture of vehicular movement and mass-meeting, one function of agri-business in these huge halls. The results are striking and much more interesting than the urban pressures of this Late-Capitalist monolith, which wants to be nothing so much as a covered shed without scale, of infinite expanse and minimum height.

Peter Eisenman, Columbus Convention Center, *1990-92. Abstract worms appear on the sides and top, while the entrance which the public use has articulated well-scaled fronts.*

A more interesting design, though unbuilt, is the house for the artist Immendorff in Dusseldorf. Here, as a concept diagram shows, two solitons – coherent waves – twist around a pick-axe shape, which is actually a fold. These are symbolically generated by forces on the site: row houses and harbour waves, which are amplified by a vortex motion. The two solitons then twist through each other, one on the outside, one on the inside. One model, made from stacked horizontals, looks like a pack of cards given several twists, but the scheme, if built, would play these off against very strong verticals, set at rotated angles. The combination of two movement systems played in counterpoint would really give the building a sense of energy, as if the two solitons were two earthquakes pushing through each other while trying to break out.

I have designed some furniture, also based on solitons going through each other, but as twists and amoeba-shapes to allow some left-over space. Here the fabrication was made simple by pretwisting the vertical structures, so the soliton appears to rise or fall: the appearance of torque is intensified by setting the verticals at a slight angle. The horizontals were also precut, rotated, then cut again at an angle so that pulses of energy appear to run throughout.

Bahram Shirdel's entry for the Nara Convention Hall (1992) uses folds rather than solitons to convey the sense of cosmogenic process: tectonic plates seem to have emerged from the ground, collided and folded over, like a slow-motion wave of dense lava. Shirdel conceives this earth-like architecture as midway between the abstract geometry of Modernism and the representational figure of Historicism. It is reminiscent of both crystalline forms of nature, geological strata,

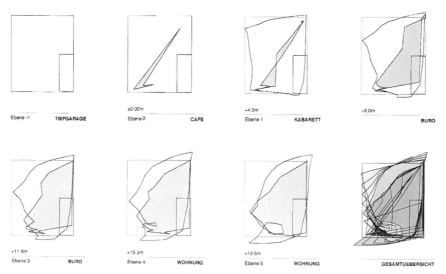

ABOVE and OVERLEAF, LEFT: Peter Eisenman, Haus Immendorf, *Dusseldorf, 1993. Two soliton waves produced by the river inlet become the pretext for architecture as frozen, twisted water, as the waves move up through each other. Computer generated grids now allow us to conceive and build such wave form architecture with some efficiency.*

and the repetitive flat surfaces of mass-production, but it also has a haunting otherness, like the best of Eisenman's work. Its hulk, its monolithic patinated-copper fractures, its self-similar Y-forms repeated at many scales, evoke an animal presence as much as a quarry. Is this Ruskinian savagery?

Shirdel makes a surprising comparison with the nearby Todaji-ji Temple in Nara, a vast Buddhist shrine which has three statues floating in its interior. Shirdel's scheme has three volumes of usable space floating below the overall enclosing, folding skin. In the old building, space is positively designed as a figural void, in the new design, space is residual – the leftover between the two generative folds of the exterior and interior. This adds to the enigmatic quality; are we back in the folded cave-spaces of Lascaux, or forward in a new disorienting shrine for theatre, music and dance? The otherness here is the present displaced.

In all these examples we can see the beginnings of a twisting, folding, wave-form architecture that still stays in one place. It represents the process of emergence through undulations, fluid and crystalline forms and calculated ambiguity; its references are multiple and between categories. The next challenge for a still more cosmogenic architecture might be to incorporate real moving parts and involve the inhabitant or viewer into a participatory relationship with objects – to do something actively which reflects the process of cosmogenesis. Architecture should engage more than the eye and thought, it should involve the other senses in motion and movement, particularly the body.

ABOVE: C Jencks, Soliton Stand, *Scotland, 1994. Waves travel through each other and flare out; shelves rotate and graduate; OVERLEAF, FROM ABOVE: Bahram Shirdel,* Nara Convention Hall, *competition entry, 1992. The flat geometry of the west elevation erupts into frozen folds as the structure rises, like tectonic plates, falling to the east. There is an uncanny scale and a feeling of rightness between architecture and crystalline fractures.*

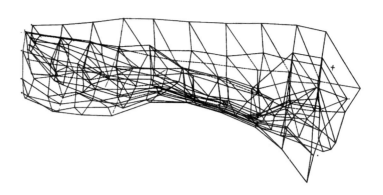

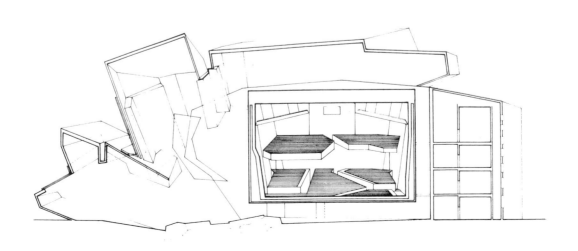

XXII
ANOTHER AESTHETIC?

Faced with too many false novelties, Mies van der Rohe said contemptuously near the end of his life: 'One cannot have a new architecture every Monday morning'. Weary of the Shock of the New, he also said: 'I'd rather be good than interesting'. The movement from creative, romantic youth to static, classical old age is a route taken by most people as they begin to know what they want and how to perfect it. Goethe's development along this line is typical.

Yet there is something false in the renunciation of an early creative ardour; a betrayal of youth, and it is something that comes naturally to an establishment, especially as it gets older. Mies was extraordinarily adaptive and creative when young: he mastered crystal glass architecture with his skyscraper projects, perfected the concrete slab office building and produced an ultimate De Stijl villa – all in the space of four years. This flexibility and invention stand opposed to the last twenty years of his life, when he worked solely on the bureaucratic office building and kept an I-beam by his desk, the perfect fetish on which to be hoisted.

A different aesthetic, from a psychological point of view, makes one see the world anew. It is akin to a rebirth, because it opens up unexplored territory, promises fresh discoveries, an unknown land. The metaphor of rebirth underlay the Renaissance, and it is ultimately spiritual, relating to conversion experiences. Today we are familiar with the 'twice-born', or 'born-again' Christian. The *locus classicus* of this experience comes from the Gospel of St John: 'except a man be born again, he cannot see the kingdom of God'. One always needs to break through the present abstractions, go beyond the language of the tribe, seek raw experience. Remember Le Corbusier's admonition: 'Eyes which do not see', the new beauty of the age. One has to be twice-born to do so. This conversion experience is so important for new sight, seeing anew, that it echoes for one hundred years from 1410-1510, as the injunction: 're-vivere, re-nasci, re-naissance'. In short, 're-birth yourself!'

Sudden insight, any small creation, can serve this role. The solving of a problem, understanding a joke, learning something surprising about the world – that time can go backwards in the quantum universe – are small versions of this conversion experience. All learning, however minor, mirrors the experience.

If the universe is forever expanding and jumping to new levels of organization, then, indeed, we need the equivalent of a new architecture every Monday morning. Or do we? It would be very difficult from a productive point of view, and absolutely exhausting for the inhabitants. Perhaps it should be rephrased: we need the continuous modification of languages and their sudden shifts.

Aesthetic codes, perceptions of beauty and sensual appearance are always partly conventional. One has to learn to see the beauty in Classical and Gothic architecture – the beauty in the New Brutalism, or the wildness of Vanbrugh. One has recently had to learn to see the beauty in ugliness and the work in the Gothic Revivalists such as William Burgess, or the kitsch of Andy Warhol, or the horror of grotesques. There is, of course, nothing in the universe that cannot be appreciated from an aesthetic point of view, and around which a taste and culture cannot form.

We know this truth as did no other generation – as well as the surprising corollary: even open-minded pluralists are repulsed by unfamiliar art and architecture. Being open-minded we have begun to distrust our revulsion; which is a pity. The historic proposition before us, which is ours to understand, is the mixed feeling of elation and anger in learning the new engenders. This mixed appreciation, of which one finds echoes in the writings of creative artists such as Picasso (especially when he is jealous of his competitors' breakthroughs), is an indication of where the cutting edge is. I should say 'edges', because there are clearly many knives being sharpened, many avenues being explored simultaneously. All the leading architects know when one in their field has made a breakthrough, and they are simultaneously jealous and delighted.

The creative edge in every field of science and art brings forth these mixed feelings. In architecture it leads to the metaphor, title of countless exhibits, 'The New Wave In . . . ' Wave indeed – it moves forward, rises, breaks, and reforms into many bits of turbulent foam, just like an architectural movement. Waves of feeling, waves of taste, waves of perception go through creator and audience alike, uniting them in exploration. The 'searchings and manifestations of the spirit', as Le Corbusier called the creative search, are momentary points reached in history when there is a unity of feeling in a culture, a spark between an artist and a community of taste. However, just as the cosmos moves and expands as it creates, so do these points constantly change and have to be re-invented.

In our over-mechanized culture, rational cognition has been, in relation to other modes of perception, overdeveloped. The philosopher Jacques Derrida reveals the consequences of this position:

[Hegel] posited that a philosophical work devoted to aesthetics, the philosophy or science of the beautiful, must exclude natural beauty. It is in everyday life that one speaks of a beautiful sky. But there is no natural beauty. More precisely, artistic beauty is superior to natural beauty, as the mind that produces it is superior to nature. One must therefore say that absolute beauty, the telos or final essence of the beautiful, appears in art and not in nature as such. [55]

ABOVE: Andy Goldsworthy, Ice, *Pennsylvania, 1992; BELOW LEFT: Stone, Monte Carlo, 1991; BELOW RIGHT: Steel, Gateshead, 1991. Natural, ephemeral and man-made materials in the external shape of the beehive dome. Nature or culture, born or made?*

Are we to deny aesthetic intention to the Bower bird, the bird that decorates its nest to attract a mate? It is clear that multiple aesthetic codes run through nature as much as culture, and if Derrida would take time off from his mind-work to visit any good aquarium he would certainly have a conversion experience: there he would find fish as flat, thin and beautiful as any good French crêpe, fish shaped like horses, and vertical fish like exclamation points. There is a greater variety of fish aesthetics than are dreamed of in our sheltered museum world. Some do not serve any function whatsoever; they are simply the results of the internal mathematics of growth, further examples of chaos dynamics producing order; aesthetic 'order for free' (as Stuart Kauffman often puts it).

Returning to the theme of a cosmogenic unfolding, we can find some sculptors exploring a naturalist language of process. Andy Goldsworthy, looking like the 'noble savage' with designer stubble and tousled jeans, goes out into the woods in the morning to discover a fitting language of expression. He finds autumnal leaves on the ground, folds and joins them in a row to form a brightly coloured chain, or pins them with pine needles into a curtain. He journeys to the north and, in one day, constructs a circular ice arch which falls the next morning. He goes to the edge of the sea and balances wet rocks precariously to a height of six feet, when the tide comes in and washes them away. His most fleeting work is to lie down spread-eagled when he sees a rain-shower coming, and let his dry after-image form: it looks very archetypal, like a Gormley sculpture squashed flat into the earth. All this ephemeral work resembles that of the ant, termite, Bower bird, or bee in at least this way: it works with a structural property that comes directly from natural materials, and it exploits this aesthetically. 'Living lightly on the earth', as ecologists advise. Letting the art perish and preserving it only in a photograph is part of his message.

The problem this would cause with architecture, however, would be increased pollution through higher rates of scrapping, in a culture which is already too throwaway. Goldsworthy's contribution to the architecture of emergence and movement is in his use of light and shadow. His stone constructions create a play of light across the surface which changes dramatically as one moves round, as light is broken up into thin, contrasting planes, almost diffraction patterns.

The American sculptor, Beverly Pepper, has pushed the naturalist aesthetic in the opposite direction: toward artifice, man-made technology, and applied ornament. Her undulating ceramic blue waves, in a Barcelona park, are naturalistic in the sense that they resemble fractals, ocean waves, clouds, and the rising and falling of the surrounding earth, but they are highly fabricated, on a reinforced concrete base. The glistening tile body, undulating up and down through the green sea of grass, is a convincing fish or reptile or living skin – a metaphor of the gestating earth it cuts through.

Such sculpture may suggest a line of development, but it is premature to speak about a developed body of cosmogenic art or architecture. That remains to be created, an important challenge for the future. What we have seen already shows that the aesthetic of movement and natural growth varies from the monumental to the ephemeral, from the classical to the anti-classical. There is no single aesthetic of nature. But, as the fishes' admonition to Derrida insists, aesthetics in the universe predated us and called our senses to order. Imagine aesthetic life on the moon, imagine a world without colour, growth, flowers, and song. The mind would be stunted, the imagination atrophied, the senses dormant.

Clearly, nature's aesthetic languages preceded and evoked our own. The fractal pattern of a fern, the Mandelbrot set discovered by a computer, the languages of mathematics expressed in a spiral shell, or the Op Art zebra are proof of that. On the other hand, culture does extend this aesthetic base with intentionality and complexity. The mind invents new aesthetic codes that may contradict and extend those already existing. In this creativity it mimics the unfolding of natural evolution, the pure expression of spirit.

Beverly Pepper, Landscape Waves, *Parc de l'Estacio del Nord, Barcelona, 1991. Blue waves rise out of the ground and disappear.*

XXIII
THE SPIRITUAL IN ARCHITECTURE: CREATIVITY IN ACTION, COSMOGENESIS IN CONTENT

There are, I believe, two opposite avenues of approach to the question of a cosmogenic architecture, each of which demands its own particular set of skills and values: one focuses on the substance of the question, the other on the language in which it is created. To illustrate this I cite a little known Czech Cubist architect, Pavel Janak, who worked and wrote just before the First World War.

In his paper 'From Modern Architecture to Architecture' (1910), Janak underscores the difference between a materialistically generated building and one created from artistic intention and form:

> Modern architects therefore behaved very materialistically, wanting to base their creations on construction and materials because the expression of construction and the animation of materials comprised a materialistically narrowed principle . . . [but] The growth of architecture as a responsive, formative and spiritual creation corresponds with the silencing of the material and construction elements and their subordination to the artistic intention. [56]

Janak goes on to defend the priority of 'space and plastic form' over materialism and practicality. Later, in an article called 'The Prism and the Pyramid', he defends the new form-language he and other Czech Cubists were evolving at the time: the crystalline, oblique form-language of spikes, angles, facets – or all those instruments that he says have evolved from 'the third force': wedges, arrows, posts, knives, and levers. The 'oblique fall of rain', he argues,

> is caused by the additional element of wind: similarly, snowdrifts, washouts, ravines, caves, sinkholes and volcanoes are, in general, either positively or negatively created forms made out of inanimate matter by another invading force, which deforms it and diverts it from the natural form in which it was deposited. [57]

In effect, dead nature created the 'bi-plane' of the horizontal and vertical, while 'animated' life 'overcame' this stasis with 'the third plane'. Hence the 'oblique' symbolized active nature and the creative will at once. For Janak this was the Baroque past of Prague and of Czech Cubism in the present.

Furthermore, prisms and pyramids were the direct expressions of the new discoveries in physics, in particular Einstein's notion of space-time connectivity wherein matter bent space and time, wherein gravity *is* geometry. All these ideas were counter-intuitive and counter-sensual. They also went directly against the Newtonian everyday world of commonsense perception. Thus a double spirituality might be achieved if the artist's will, or *kunstwollen*, could overcome dead form with new oblique shapes *and* represent the cosmic truths behind misleading appearances. Czech Cubists did this with an outburst of creative willpower that touched every area.

Buildings had sloping planes and cut-off corners; furniture had peaked hats and sometimes knocked-kneed legs, as if it were buckling under the weight of the form. Crockery looked like folded paper or a crystal multiplying itself; cabinets were hitched in at the waist and bowed out at the shoulders; clocks looked like fractured alpine landscapes; chandeliers like mountain peaks. Indeed, the peaked V-form, pyramid, and prism – rather than the cube of Cubism – were the leading motifs that cut across all surfaces, utensils, posters and even clothes.

It is clear from all this that Janak and several other Czech Cubists saw a new spiritual architecture emerging both from contemporary science and Cubist invention, the substance of a new cosmology (as revealed by Einstein and Bergson), and a new language. He understood the twin and opposite commitments that the architect must make, and his architecture and furniture show that he could translate this into a fresh, if primitive, creativity.

Unfortunately, the Czech Cubists' period of creativity was cut short by war and later by the rise of the International Style and Functionalism. But the impulse of a cosmological spirituality, rooted in new languages of form and the new sciences, jumped across Europe, and even became the heart of the early Bauhaus. Tragically it did not survive the Modernism, materialism, and scepticism of the 1920s. Malevich spoke for it and was self-silenced; Johannes Itten made it the foundation of the Bauhaus and was forced out; Mondrian, Klee, and

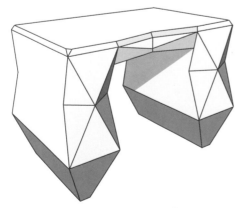 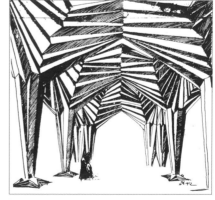

FROM LEFT TO RIGHT: Pavel Janak, Writing Desk, *design, 1912. Crystal Czech cubism; Pavel Janak,* Monumental Interior, *design, India Ink, 1912, NTM collection No 85. Janak. Between architecture and landscape and crystal.*

151

Kandinsky based their abstraction on similar theories but then suppressed them.

Le Corbusier was himself a partial victim. In the early 1920s he extolled the 'new spirit' (*Esprit Nouveau*) and wrote that we can directly apprehend the harmonies in the universe because of a common resonance:

> [harmonious proportions] arouse, deep within us and beyond our sense, a resonance, a sort of sounding-board which begins to vibrate. An indefinable trace of the Absolute which lies in the depth of our being. This sounding-board which vibrates in us is our criterion of harmony. This is indeed the axis on which man is organized in perfect accord with nature and probably with the universe . . . [58]

For Le Corbusier the 'spirit' was more mental than spiritual, but, in any case, by the late 1920s he was forced to fight on a reductivist and functionalist front, as the Machine Age rolled in from Germany over another of its spiritual prophets. Walter Gropius also followed this trajectory, jumping from his lively perorations and Expressionism of 1919, to his sober, no-nonsense grid-locks of 1928. Janak's crystalline forms, Itten's spirals, Malevich's abstractions, Kandinsky's cosmic formalism, Gropius' expressionism and Le Corbusier's pure forms were differently inspired, but nonetheless they shared a common agenda in opposing a lifeless academicism. The life of forms in art, and the spirit of emergence behind this

Charles Jencks, Fractal Dome, *Scotland, 1992.*

life, embodied a new ethic of creativity. For a short time it was understood as such, perhaps an unconscious expression of an emergent Post-Christianity.

But then the argument was cut short. Modernists decided to make their peace with mass-production, a consumer society, the power structure and one crisis in Europe after another – inflation, depression and fascism. Perhaps much of this settlement was unavoidable but, in any case, the materialist paradigm finally silenced the notion of spirituality as the creative exploration of new languages – imagination in action.

It also suppressed the nature of the new cosmogenesis and its spiritual implications. Indeed, even Einstein himself could not face the implications of his own theories of relativity and, in what he called the 'greatest blunder of my life', introduced data to suppress the evidence of an open, creative, unfolding universe. He preferred a mechanistic, deterministic, materialistic, reductivist universe to the one contained in his own theories. He preferred Newton to Einstein!

Such is the power of a reigning paradigm.

It is time to reclaim this historic territory from the materialist trap and save the Modernists from the dark side of their own world view: time to insist that, before the taboos set in, their early work was spiritual and understood to be so. However, there is a problem of words here. One can well understand their growing reluctance to speak of things spiritual and their 'Negative Theology', most pronounced in the philosopher Wittgenstein. One can see that so much spirituality turned into spiritualism and New Age mumbo-jumbo. One can see that the word 'spiritual' is contaminated, hijacked by the media and often used as an excuse not to think. All of this is true, but still not enough to justify the suppression of what was discovered: the idea that artists and architects, by continuously creating and basing their content on discoveries of science and cosmology, were engaged in a spiritual search. Perhaps we do need a new word for this.

At all events, things have changed; there is a new paradigm and it is most evident in the Post-Modern sciences of complexity that have now sublated the Modern sciences of simplicity. It is only a matter of time before this new paradigm spreads to the academies and becomes an orthodoxy. This will not be without its problems, but the problems will be more benign than those of the materialist world view, for the new theory will force us to focus at the same time on two areas: the developing story of cosmogenesis and the creative use of new languages which stem from it.

XXIV
RECAPTURING THE BAUHAUS SPIRIT: YALP

When he founded the Bauhaus in 1919, Walter Gropius projected a strong, romantic confidence, reflecting his past as a much-decorated cavalry officer in the First World War and a successful practising architect before it. Photographs of him at the time reveal why Paul Klee christened him 'the Silver Prince': he was aristocratically handsome, and when he trained his intense, melancholic stare at one he was hypnotic – a charmed prince. Some found him the very presence of a mystic and, during the four annual Bauhaus festivals, it was not unknown for him to adopt the role of a spiritual Father Christmas. He would take students into the woods and sing and dance for them, like a wood sprite, or, as a student Gunta Stolzl recounts:

> Christmas was indescribably beautiful, something quite new, a 'Festival of Love' in every detail. A beautiful tree, lights and apples, a long white table, big candles, beautifully laid, a big fir wreath, everything green. Under the tree everything white, on it countless presents. Gropius read the Christmas story, Emma Heim sang. We were all given presents by Gropius, so kind and lovely and special to every Bauhausler. Then a big meal. All in a spirit of celebration and a sense of the symbolism. Gropius served everyone their food in person. Like the washing of feet.[59]

While this view of the spiritual Bauhaus, and its Christ-like leader, may suggest a solemn air, the actual mood was anarchic, humorous, exhilarating. Not only were there riotous festivals, celebrated with the people of Weimar, in which everyone dressed up in theatrical costumes, but everyday life at the new school was an exercise in Dada invention, heavy breathing exercises, the eating of much garlic, and the creation of practical jokes as art. Gropius put costume balls, music, poetry, theatre and communal ceremonies at the heart of his Bauhaus Manifesto. He was the center of a circus of creation, and he loved it.

However, towards the end of his life, when I met him he looked dejected, even depressed. I do not know whether it was the pressure of old age, his habitual demeanour, or perhaps my presence as a harbinger of post-modernism, but when I saw him at the Harvard Graduate School of Design in 1962 he was shuffling around with grim visage – set in a depressed mask midway between a noble gravitas and pained boredom. I asked myself, 'could this be the founder of the Bauhaus – what went wrong?'

Read the ringing exhortation of his Expressionist manifesto quoted in the first chapter and you can hear the youthful passion: 'build in fantasy without regard for technical difficulties. To have the gift of imagination is more important than all technology, which always adapts itself to man's creative will' (see p20 and note 3). These are not the words of the man I saw, beaten down by too many responsibilities of architectural practice, or, as I might now surmise, of someone locked into an economic production-line.

When I knew Gropius he was still the titular head of TAC – The Architects' Collaborative – a moderately successful office set up with students, professors and designers from the Cambridge, Massachusetts area. They had work around the world – in Baghdad, London, Germany, Greece – and were designing big corporate buildings such as the Pan Am skyscraper right above Grand Central Station in New York City, ground zero of the capitalist world. Gropius had the kind of practice, and success, that any architect might want, and yet he did not look pleased. Worse still, and since anyone's face can be deceptive, the buildings of TAC looked extremely unhappy – frigid, uncreative, uptight, conformist – what, at the time of *The Man in the Grey Flannel Suit*, was called 'businessman's vernacular'.

Somewhere along the line, Gropius had sold out to the pressures of big business, the regularities of *homo economicus*. I did not know of his appeals to the Nazis in 1933, nor his compromised design for the Reichsbank – the attempted accommodation to power – nor, by contrast, did I know just how creative the early Bauhaus was, from 1919 to 1926 (but particularly the first three years). These truths emerged to me slowly, as they became more accessible through new books and exhibitions. It was only when I became involved in a BBC film celebrating seventy-five years of the Bauhaus, looked more deeply into the accounts of the Bauhauslers and saw what they were actually producing in the basic *Vorkurs*, Theatre workshop and annual spring festivals, that I began to see there was a hidden logic to their enterprise. The famous 'idea of the Bauhaus', which every head of the institute, from Gropius to Mies, mentioned, and nobody explained, rested on a principle that sounds too banal to enunciate. I have spelled it backwards, above: yalp – play, creative play.

Yes. This secret of the Bauhaus was formulated by Johannes Itten in his preliminary *Vorkurs,* and given as his mantra which every student had to learn before progressing through the school: 'Play becomes party – party becomes work – work becomes play'. This daily cycle of play-work took place under a very unusual man, and hardly the one we associate with a functionalist Bauhaus style. Itten was a man who designed his own clothes; monks' robes of the Mazdaznan sect with primitive cosmic symbols of the sun and moon, a man who would warm up classes in basic design with breathing and meditation exercises. These would free the students' creativity.

During the short German inflationary period, when there was no money for materials and tools, students would rummage through waste heaps and concoct designs from different materials – scrap metal, discarded machines, used-clothes, whatever. One should emphasize that such play with second-hand nature was directed by new visual systems and spiritual logics, the colour theory and compositional technique borrowed from Expressionist painters, and the spirituality inspired by a host of sects in Europe at the time: Theosophy, Anthroposophy, and Mazdaznanism. Otherwise it sounds amateurish, New Age, all sandals and veggie – which of course it was in part; most students reeked of garlic. What lifted it above this plane was the inspiration and intelligence of the masters – Gropius, Klee, Kandinsky, Schlemmer, Feininger – and the inspirational ideology; the idea that a new spiritual culture could be formed at Weimar that would lead the world, and a specific set of artistic problems would be solved. The sense of purpose, one can hear behind every Gropius proclamation, was to create a new visual and spiritual culture. The intention mattered, the masters mattered, the moment mattered – but all of it would have come to nothing without explorative play.

This point can also be inferred from negative examples: the failure of subsequent Bauhauses which were attempted in Chicago, at Rocky Mountain College and Ulm, or even Harvard and other design schools. It never worked again, partly of course because the mix and moment were never right but also because the theory had been lost: yalp.

Clearly it is not a *sufficient* theory of artistic creation; John Dewey and other educators have emphasized the same principle, and their lesson has not been fully absorbed, either. Perhaps this is because it has to be countered by search and exploration, goal-directed research on particular subjects. The process of creation, as Arthur Koestler has shown in *The Act of Creation* (1964), demands at least two opposite aspects of the personality: critical reasoning and dreaming aside. These complementary aspects, as Coleridge pointed out in his famous discussion of Imagination (see pp39-40 and note 11), produce 'a more than usual state of emotion, with more than usual order', or a work poised between order and entropy. The role of play in the creative process is to free up the habitual links between things and allow new ones to occur; the role of directed research is to provide an ordering principle. So, in a successfully creative institution, or individual, both these contrary impulses have to be cultivated.

At the Bauhaus, the ordering principle was served by the various workshops and their particular tasks and, at the institution as a whole, the hunt for a series of new form languages, new styles. But here there is a problem. Walter Gropius had condemned the idea of 'a Bauhaus Style' as a contradiction in terms, the admission of defeat. This condemnation caused confusion because, so clearly to others, the life of the institution was manifest in its pursuit of a fresh aesthetic – or rather, and this may clarify the confusion, aesthetics. Perhaps Gropius was only censoring the idea of a single style.

Be that as it may, and coming back to our main theme, why should explorative play be so important? Because it is directly connected to evolution, learning, the unfolding of new ideas and events. This is why a creative institution, such as the Bauhaus, or a creative architect, such as Frank Gehry, has so much power. We naturally find creative work fascinating, gripping, sexy, mesmerizing, spiritual, addictive, humorous – and a host of related qualities – because it represents the growth of the mind responding to the evolution of the cosmos; to a basic force of the universe.

According to Complexity Theory, 'complex adaptive systems' (or learning systems) can be found throughout nature, from the very small to the very large. We take the omnipresence and importance of learning much too much for granted, probably because our schools are more factories for training than places where learning is enjoyed. We pay lip-service to the notion of education, while being privately bored by the idea. We acknowledge that the countries which will prosper in the twenty-first century, when the global knowledge economy becomes yet more powerful, will be those which place priority on education: we admit all

FROM LEFT TO RIGHT: Johannes Itten, Tower of Fire, Wood and Coloured Glass*, Weimar, 1992 – the depiction of cosmic jumps? (Bauhaus Archive, Berlin); Frank Gehry,* Guggenheim Museum*, Bilbao, 1994 model – creating the next jump.*

this, just before we cut education budgets.

The Anglo-Saxons were the first to recognize that education pays dividends – the English and American empires were built on this truth – and then, under Thatcher and Reagan, were the first to de-skill, de-educate and 'dumb down' much of their population.

Learning is the basic drive of the universe, far more powerful than sex and almost on an equal footing with eating. The reason is that it, too, is directly connected with survival. If one eats well mentally, one will live tomorrow and even prosper. This fact is known all the way from the humble amoeba to the collective brains known as neural-nets and connected computers. There are four basic levels of evolutionary learning: the prebiotic chemical (such things as catalytic peptides and catalytic RNA), the biological (such things as ecosystems and immune systems), the individual human (such things as school work and apprenticeship), and the cultural (the evolution of societies, the global economy and computer strategies). [60]

If complex adaptation is a fundamental drive and if explorative play is necessary for creative enterprise, it is also essential that the combination – dynamic learning – is directed at the most important issue we face: the nature of the cosmos. What better subjects for our playful art and architecture than the laws of the universe and our new view of nature, subjects to which we will now turn.

XXV
THE RETURN TO A DIFFERENT NATURE

In the next fifty years, according to conservative predictions, we will rebuild nature. Or, to put it more exactly, we will build more architecture, cities, roads, suburbs, defence systems, and communications networks – second nature – than have all preceding civilizations put together. That fact is momentous, but small compared to the possible ecological implications. As we have seen, when an earth-system such as Gaia is pushed far from equilibrium some runaway growth is inevitable. We do not know what it will be, although we can guess it will not be particularly kind to the remaining species. The basic truth cannot be denied: when energy, information, pollution, or *any* quantity is continuously added, all self-organizing systems jump to new levels – remember the sandpile? (see p86).

Furthermore, and as if the foregoing were not enough, the boundaries between nature and culture, or the external biological world and the constructed world, will, with genetic engineering and cyborgs, become completely blurred.

The two trends are interconnected – increasing knowledge and increasing transformation of resources – and they necessitate a shift from the Modernists' view of nature. Nature is *not* something distinct from us; we are thoroughly enmeshed in the emergent properties of the universe. While we have more or less stopped evolving physically, we have just begun to evolve techno-biologically. If our buildings, as I have argued, reflect our world views, we must modify them to come closer to what we now know about the universe – its nonlinearity, emergence, complexity and self-organization. Otherwise we will go on building an alienated environment and contribute to Gaia's decline. Negatively, we are the first generation to be forced by population pressures to go cosmogenic; positively, we are the first to be drawn by a new vision of emergence.

Modernism, to reiterate, *did* open some doors – to greater democracy, progressive technology and critical freedom – and also the main vista to cosmic speculation. Copernicus, Newton and Darwin changed our view of nature and our place in it for good; but also, very much, for 'bad'. As to the former, we left the center of a static system and arrived in a suburban location on a minor galaxy, the Milky Way, in a local cluster which is part of a small wall of galaxies. Galileo also showed that the earth, not the sun, was the moving satellite; as he said after being persecuted by the Vatican – '*and still it moves*'. All this was true, if denting to our ego.

However, Newton then provided us with the mechanistic view of nature's laws, and so we saw Her as an extremely complex kind of clock. Darwin further eroded our view of a beneficent nature and our place in it – first cousin to the

159

aggressive apes – followed by the Modernist of our century, Sigmund Freud, who adopted the mechanical view of the psyche as a set of forces and levers (ego, super-ego, id). The Freudian world view presented a human nature driven by instinctual forces that overpower reason, grace, and sensitivity.

The Evolution of Second Nature

As we have seen, with the new sciences of complexity we now know the universe is more like the self-repairing, self-transforming butterfly than the nineteenth-century machine. Moreover, the cybernetic machine, with its changing software as the driving force, is losing its mechanical *nature*. In ten years' time the word and concept 'machine' will be self-contradictory because it will have become creative, anticipatory, non-routine – that is, non-mechanical.

Today, when an organ or limb wears out or is injured, people are given a prosthetic device – a plastic hip, or mechanical leg. These mechanisms are equipped with microprocessors which can respond sensitively to pressures on the skin: they are keyed into the nervous system so they can move this way or that, on impulse. In America, twelve thousand people have had their brains 'wired up' with ear implants to restore hearing.[61] Some blind people are beginning to be able to see again with analogous systems of microtechnology plugged into the brain.

Over the last ten years, fifteen thousand people worldwide have had electronic components hooked up to their nervous systems: the age of *Homo cyborg* – where animal and technology are fully integrated – has arrived. Significantly, no one wired up with these prosthetic devices feels any the less human, or like a robot. Quite the contrary, they feel more human because they are more empowered to do what they want. The cybernated machine has become second nature and slipped below consciousness. The nervous system has absorbed and integrated the smart-machine, just as it does when one rides a bicycle.

Because of the new software, the 'Modernist trap' – the spectre of the first chapter – will be able to jump. We will enter the age of more liberated machines, machines that can talk, walk and think. According to theorists of evolutionary technology, such as Kevin Kelly, the new bio-machines will think small and sensitively, and that will change our notions of mechanism into anti-mechanism. The fact that a machine can now beat the world's best chess player, Kasparov, is not the point. That victory was the result of computing power, number-crunching, no more surprising than the fact that a mechanical digger can lift more earth than a weightlifter. It is not a human failing that Kasparov cannot think out, in a second, the next 100,000 moves, but rather a victory for our designed computers.

Even 'thinking' machines, neural-net computers that can fool people into thinking they are alive, do not diminish our self-image. Until we send one through school, introduce it to society, tell it to joke – that is until it can learn to understand why the world is as it is and feel the significance of history, art and politics – it will fail to understand the rudiments of thought. Even if we do send a cyborg to college we have nothing to envy because, if it did have the proper sentiments, it would suffer the Frankenstein syndrome: lonely, and furious that it was not organic like normal people. There is great cause for hope in the evolution of machines towards us. This is another instance of increasing complexity, of progress in sensitivity, delicacy, discrimination, and doing more with less (although again there are dangerous implications).

All the indications are that second nature – technology and industrialization – is growing too fast. Ecological stress shows that culture and civilization are becoming too big with respect to the biosphere, the carrying capacity of earth. Although no nation is willing to admit the fact, it looks as if we are reaching the global limits of economic growth. In any case, as pointed out on pages 91-93, it is absolutely clear that, because of the destruction of habitats and of 27,000 species per year, we will have to manage the nature we have inherited; that is, first nature. Management is not altogether an attractive prospect, because it puts us into an instrumental relationship with nature, a form of alienation.

Instead of being able to enjoy, and identify with a bountiful background – the mountains, seas and plains – we will have to control, garden and domesticate them. Otherwise habitats and species will perish at an even greater rate. Given our respective sizes, management is not desirable but necessary. There is an argument that, when the human population grew to over 500 million, as it did after the industrial revolution, stewardship of the earth became inevitable. This

 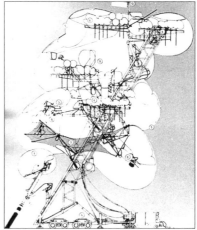

Cyborg Architecture *was mooted in the 1960s, with schemes by Coop Himmelblau and others. Their* Cloud, *1968-72, was a mobile, responsive architecure like a prosthetic device connected to an organism allowing feedback. 'Coop Himmelblau' means 'the idea of having architecture with fantasy, as buoyant and variable as clouds' – they, like many other 60s characters, were too early.*

may explain attitudes developed in the Bible. When, in *Genesis*, it calls for us to have 'dominion over the beasts', it is framing an ecological imperative. Our 'Original Sin' is having grown too large.[62] Species extinction started 10,000 years ago with the Neolithic Revolution, and that is our fall from grace, our expulsion from the Garden of Eden. Whatever we make of this mythic interpretation, the fact of management ties us into first nature much more closely than ever before. We will even decide what is to remain 'wild', and therefore wilderness itself will end up in a national park or, worse, theme park.

Not Reductivism but Elevationism

Another emergent truth, which ties us into nature much more profoundly than the Modernists, is the discovery that the principle of self-organization extends everywhere from the atom to the universe as a whole. Christian mystics may have known this truth in the thirteenth century; Romantic poets and philosophers may have revived it in the nineteenth: and Buddhists never doubted it for a moment. But the broad picture in the West has been that we are separate from nature, and superior to it, in volition, intelligence, freedom and spirit. Nature – a stone or quarry – was considered a dead and mechanical thing. Its elements were like a chair or carriage, functional objects, things which definitely had no internal qualities.

Yet a basic truth of quantum physics has been that the atom is itself an ecological entity with internal properties of organization. The electron, orbiting the nucleus as both wave and particle, jumps from quantum level to level, giving off, or taking on, energy. Its behaviour is partly self-determined and partly indeterminant. The electron cloud is said to 'choose' certain aspects of its activity, just as we 'choose' whether to observe its position or momentum, particle or wave aspect. Its freedoms and our freedoms are circumscribed, but we both exhibit a degree of self-determinism and interaction. Consequently, we treat it with more respect than an unorganized, dead piece of matter. Quantum physics has shown us many different 'life-like' aspects of the atom – its fuzziness, dynamism, and quixotic thought-like behaviour. As mentioned above, many scientists, such as Roger Penrose, believe that our thought has a quantum component. All these parallels between us and the ultimate particles of reality tie us and first nature more directly to each other.

There is yet another sense in which we are becoming much more deeply embedded in nature by the Post-Modern sciences of complexity. The atomic world is taking over the role which used to be given to our bodies. The Ancient Greek philosopher Protagoras formulated the old standard of measurement which lasted for 2,500 years: 'man is the measure of all things'. This maxim was taken to heart, particularly in the Renaissance when many buildings, and their details, were derived through human proportions. Legal definitions of the foot and inch were derived from our variable frame, which was averaged out and then set at an arbitrary dimension. Even as recently as 1960, Le Corbusier based his measurement sequence, known as the Modulor, on a six-foot high Englishman, because, in his reading of crime fiction, the British detective is always that height. In 1875, the Treaty of the Meter tried to put a bit of common order and sense into variable measures, and established the international standard units for the second, the kilogram and the meter (fixing the inch at 2.54 centimeters, exactly). The platinum and iridium prototype meter is kept in a temperature-controlled strong room, which can only be opened by the simultaneous use of three different keys turned by trusted officials.

Now things have changed. All fundamental measures, except the kilogram, have been put on a much more exact and universal basis as they are redefined in cosmic terms. Instead of measuring days, hours, minutes and seconds by the wobbly, erratic turns of the earth, it has been put on the more regular atomic standard. A caesium clock has, since 1967, redefined the basic measure of the second as the duration of 9,192,631,770 cycles of atomic radiation. Since 1983, the meter has been redefined by international agreement as the distance that light travels through a vacuum, ie, in $^1/_{299,792,458}$ of a second. Thus the ultimate unit of space is derived from an atomic unit of time – a convergence of space-time universality – and some day soon weight will also fall to the quantum standard. As the physicist Hans Christian von Baeyer states: 'In the twenty-first century the atom will replace man as the measure of all things.' [63] The cosmos will be the standard for us, and all the rest of nature.

Thus we are going cosmic not just because the earth is in crisis and pollution is forcing us to do so, but because our culture is now adopting the standards of the universe. Here we are close to what Stephen Hawking believes is 'seeing the mind of God'. As Paul Davies put it in *The Mind of God*, the laws of nature turn

Charles Jencks, Paul Davies, Equations which Generate the World *(constructed by Brookbrae), Scotland, 1994.*

out to have most of the attributes of a Christian God: they are universal (apply everywhere in the universe), absolute (do not depend on anything else), eternal (do not change with time), omnipotent (all-powerful), and creative of the universe (cosmogenic).[64]

Some scientists and philosophers believe that these laws are social constructions; that we invent mathematical models which just happen to be useful in describing regularities. Yet most scientists believe they are discovering something objectively real and that reality 'obeys' or is 'subject to' these laws. With Peter Fuller, Roger Penrose and the few other New Platonists around, I also believe this transcendent realm exists. Its importance is not only to set the universe in motion and sustain it but, as far as we are concerned, to be a measure and standard for us – independent of us. Because the laws illustrate this otherness, I have chosen to design them into and onto buildings, in both literal equations and performative figures.

In effect the relations between us and first and second nature are being renegotiated all at once. External reality – growing nature and cyborg machines – are being pulled in our direction. Human nature is typical of all self-organization and we can find counterparts to all our passions – good and bad – in the growing field of ethology (the study of animals in their natural habitat).

We have moved from being cut off and above nature to being 'typical of the best'. This has benign consequences. Instead of Modernist reductivism which reduced us to a mechanism, we have elevated machines into cyborgs, that is towards our position of creative freedom. And instead of Christian snobbism, which said we were superior to all other beings who did not have a soul, we have elevated other species as we have discovered their volition, languages, even cultures. In short, the Post-Modern, holistic view of the universe has turned Modern and Christian reductivisms on their head and upgraded the rest of nature with a new view. This could be called elevationism because it looks for human qualities in everything. The implications are that everything has a sacred component and some final worth – or intrinsic quality – for itself.

That we are deeply embedded in the rest of nature and grow out of deep cosmic processes is also a consequence of the predispositionist view of the universe. This, to reiterate, contends that given the laws of the universe, things like us will inevitably evolve. As Freeman Dyson has written: 'The universe knew we were coming'.[64] In effect the universe, as a cosmogenic process, is trying to produce 'human-like-stuff' and, in terms of intelligence, shape other things more like us. In this sense we are the measure of one part of universe activity, one measure of where it has evolved after fifteen billion years of marching up the complexity-sensitivity-intelligence scale. But this *does* create anxiety over the next step, which we can well imagine: the new man of Nietzsche and the Futurists. Protean man – 'something more than man' or, better, something more intensely wo-manly. Will the next species be more intensely, ultra-us?

We could guess that any sentient being evolving from us will become involved in the great speculation of trying to figure out the rules and processes of cosmogenesis, trying to catch up, or stay ahead. It may be in the end a vain pursuit, but it is a noble one.

New Roles

The extreme consciousness of our various possible futures leads to the anxiety of over-choice, the quandary of the consumer paralyzed in the supermarket with an *embarrass de richesses*. Since we cannot know the future but do understand the way it will be created through sudden organizational jumps, we might follow the strategy shown by cosmogenesis: maximize the alternative models of growth. As we have seen in the last chapter, learning through trying different emergent models is the basic trusted method. That is why we must examine the different architectures of the jumping universe. None is sufficient alone; only the array. It varies from organic to fractal architecture, folded structures to wave-buildings, moving structures to ones that represent change, anthropomorphic to zoomorphic, ecological to organi-tech, cyborg to cosmogenic.

We must steer a course between two historical traps: the Modernist, which cut us off from nature and the Pantheist, which tried to assimilate us into it. The latter overlooked the entropy and destructiveness in cosmogenesis. It also underrated the kitsch and repetitive stereotyping apparent in many a flower, fractal or crystal. Gaia shows us, and Complexity Theory explains, the overproduction, waste and runaway growth in first nature. What could be called 'critical ecology' might be an acknowledgement of this and a response to Deep Ecology, Social Ecology and Eco-Feminism. It would admit the occasional nastiness of nature which Darwin revealed, but nevertheless celebrate the goodness, beauty and variety which are as essential. Critical ecology takes a mental effort. But the distinction has its counterpart in classical religions which have recognized and thematized principles of cosmic evil and destruction (Shiva, the devil) and seen them as being as essential to the universe as positive qualities.

How different is our new view of nature and our place in it? We are much more embedded in nature and the universe than the Modernists believed, but also we are enmeshed in the 'evil' processes of ancient myths. We find cyborgs evolving inside us and outside of us and becoming more sensitive like us. This is a second nature which we build from a nanotechnology that mimics first nature.

The distinctions between being born and being made are disappearing, those between first nature, culture and second nature are dissolving. We have returned to the nature that the Romantics loved but find it is quite different. Our qualities are both in it and in the new organi-machines. Good and 'evil', truth and lies, beauty and kitsch are really 'out there' and 'in here'.

We find ourselves in an unfinished universe, some fifteen billion years old, as co-creators. This is partly an interventionist role for us. The earth needs us to fend off possible catastrophes; the comets and asteroids of mass-destruction that can, if their path is seen far enough ahead, be deflected, possibly by nuclear explosions. It also needs us to intervene against ourselves, to get our economies under control, or to improve nature where it is blind, stupid and nasty. No doubt in this managerial role we will blunder since, as we now know, the Butterfly Effect will have its way – tiny interventions will be magnified hugely and unpredictably. But there is no escape from intervention. We long ago passed the fatal point of interaction with the globe: we went cosmic and were locked into a fearful embrace. The only hope is to learn faster than our mistakes run away with us – a race of two positive feedbacks on a jumping planet.

As co-creators we begin to understand that nature and culture are often best changed, not through coercion, but rather persuasion, play and wonder – the learning arts. This is a consequence of the basic truth that all of nature is an adaptive, self-organizing entity. It is always trying to learn its situation, compute the next move of the universe (which the universe does not know).

While we can discern an overall positive direction to the universe, towards complexity and increasing sensitivity, it is a trend accompanied by horrific exceptions. The main story is benign, but the fine print horrific. A tragic optimism is forced upon us, one that acknowledges this mixed verdict of cosmogenesis. To reflect it adequately, the architecture of the jumping universe will be various but motivated by the duality – optimism and tragedy. Einstein once said the most important question you can ask is: 'Is the universe a good place?' Yes, and it can be better if we understand, love and criticize it better.

FROM LEFT TO RIGHT: The array of cosmic architecture from organi-tech to the protected urban garden, Santiago Calatrava and Jean Nouvel.

XXVI
CRITERIA FOR ARCHITECTURE

What are the implications of the new view of cosmogenesis for architecture? What, after all, is to be done at this particular place in cultural time? One conclusion follows the Complexity Theory which has an ironic implication for a polemic – there are no simple answers. Nevertheless there are definite directions implied, as well as positive and negative trends for orientation. Certain things are demanded, others are placed in doubt, and a few questions are left open or undecidable. There is some latitude for architectural principles in the age of complexity, and they are necessarily unfinished because of the principle of emergence, and contingently unfinished because of my limitations and focus. Nonetheless, here are eight directions which follow our situation and argument.

Building close to nature and natural languages. Natural forms tie us into the cosmos at one end of the continuum, cyborgs tie us in at the other, so design should face both ways. Design, therefore, with twists and folds, waves and fractals, self-similarity instead of exact repetition. Look to the rhetoric of natural systems such as crystals, bones, slime-mould and clouds. Such forms represent continuity with the natural world, and it might be supplemented with an additional source of creativity; that is, ourselves as the originators of a second nature.

Representation of the basic cosmogenic truth – self-organization, emergence and jumps to a higher (or lower) level. There is a basic direction of evolution towards increasing complexity, but it is attained through an oppositional process of gradual improvement and catastrophic change, continuity and jumps, smooth transitions and the Butterfly Effect. The universe story is fundamentally one of unpredictability and surprise. Architecture might therefore dramatize punctuated equilibrium, the optimism and tragedy; and it can do this through both juxtaposition and smooth continuity.

Organizational depth, multivalence, complexity and the edge of chaos. Evolution pushes species, the mind and machines towards the edge of chaos, and it

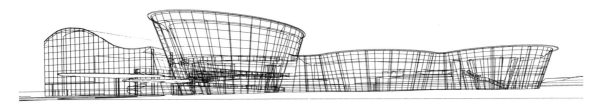

Kisho Kurokawa, Fukui City Museum of Art, *1994. Smooth transitions and the suppleness of clouds.*

is the most fruitful place to be. The creative modes which achieve depth are imaginative play and intellectual research, while the rhetorical means are redundancy, self-similarity, variation on themes, feedback, and rich linkage. A too-simple order is boring, an overly-connected building is too complicated, so one looks for an upper mean of connections. The injunction is not New Age – 'connect, always connect everything', nor traditional – 'order the chaos'; but rather 'higher organization out of order *and* chaos'.

The celebration of diversity, variety, bottom-up participatory systems which maximize difference. Since 'more is different', watch when systems grow in size, energy, information and start to jump, for then there is opportunity for change. Since the universe cannot compute its own next move, the only sensible policy is to have as much diversity as possible. Diversity creates tension and conflict, but these are small prices to pay for continuous evolution. If the universe as a whole, and societies as parts, are inherently self-organizing and in the end chaotic, the survival strategy will depend on a variety of models, species and approaches. The conclusion must be that one should foster a difference which will reach a maximum point of 'self-organizing criticality'; that is, just before it explodes in complication.

Diversity can be supported by techniques such as collage, radical eclecticism and superposition. The equivalence of age and depth can be built into a house or city by including a mixture of different designers in a single scheme, or by using methods which simulate this heterogeneity. The juxtaposition and superposition of different systems is superior to the minimalist method of excluding variety.

Architecture should acknowledge the time and its compelling agenda, which include the ecological imperative and political pluralism. This truth leads to the various green alternatives and locally-based styles which root a building in a particular time, place and constructional relevance. We cannot deny the mass-extinctions which are caused indirectly by modernization. Architecture may be powerless to change this situation directly but, like any cultural practice, it can change consciousness by symbolizing the situation and proposing a piecemeal alternative. However, since architecture is always more than its agenda . . .

It should have a double-coding of these concerns with aesthetic and conceptual codes. Most building tasks are complex, not simple, and demand a mixed response which takes on the opposed requirements of history, urbanism, contrary function and differing tastes. Since all architecture is coded, and experienced through a language of architecture, it owes as much obligation to the formal system as to the content. As the public language of the environment, architecture must adopt a shared symbolism and this means both the local and universal, cosmogenic language.

Architecture must look to science, especially contemporary sciences, for disclosures of the Cosmic Code. To get beyond the provincial concerns of the moment, beyond anthropomorphism and fashion, to regain a power that all great architecture has had, it must look to the transcendent laws which science reveals. The shared content of architecture lies primarily in these laws: such things as the priority of wave motion which is fundamental to thought, to our being, to the quantum world and perhaps to an ultimate reality of superstrings. However, right content, like right-thinking, is not enough. A cosmogenic architecture must embody imagination in action, it must dramatize creative processes, or it is nothing. Its spiritual role is to portray the laws and be emergent – that is surprise.

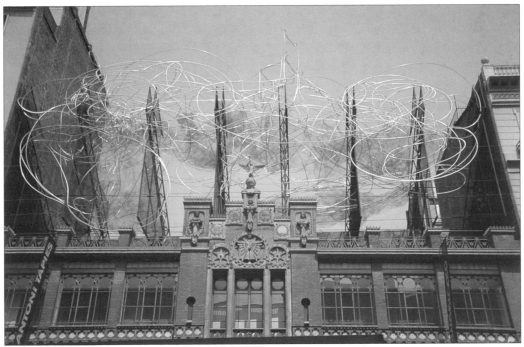

Wave Cloud/Particle Line – *the image of superstrings? Antoni Tapies, Barcelona, 1990.*

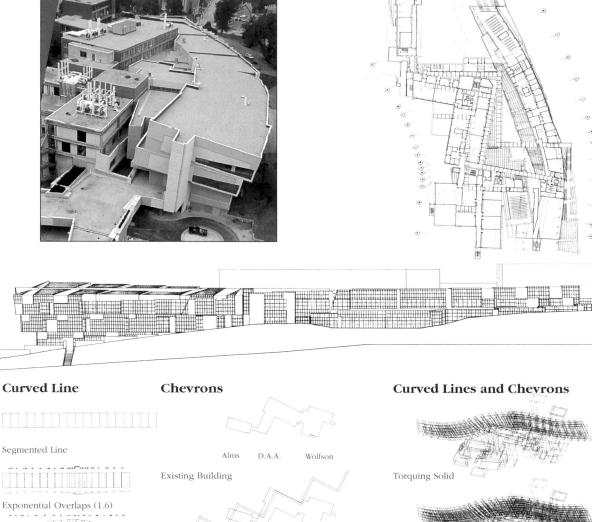

Curved Line

Segmented Line

Exponential Overlaps (1.6)

Asymptotic Tilts (1.2)

Vertical Stepping

Exponential Torque (1.1)

Phase Shift

Chevrons

Alms   D.A.A.   Wolfson

Existing Building

Ideal Chevron

Trace of Existing Building Aligned with Wolfson

Trace of Existing Building Aligned with Alms

Curved Lines and Chevrons

Torquing Solid

Torquing Solid and Trace

Torquing Solid and Trace, Stepping Solid

Torquing Solid and Trace, Stepping Solid and Trace

Peter Eisenman (with Lorenz and Williams), Aronoff Center of Design and Art, *University of Cincinnati, 1989-96. Staccato segments wrap into existing zig-zags – a new urban grammar of contextualism generated by overlaps, torques, chevrons, steps and oscillating waves.*

170

POSTSCRIPT:
ARCHITECTURE BECOMES LAND-FORM

Since the first edition of this book, written in 1994, the complexity paradigm has continued to develop and gather strength. Three major buildings of the early 1990s are finished or nearly so (those by Peter Eisenman, Daniel Libeskind and Frank Gehry) and work by lesser known architects (Enric Miralles, Zvi Hecker, the groups ARM and Ushida Findlay Partnership) has widened this growing tradition. While it cannot be said to dominate professional practice – thankfully no approach does – it is moving into a central position without losing vigor. This sustained, broadening creativity is one of its most promising aspects. Most successful traditions today soon fall apart. As I mentioned in Chapter XIX, quite a few High-Tech architects arc flirting with the paradigm and one of the best of them, Nicholas Grimshaw, has complex structures nearing completion. Complexity Building, Cosmogenic Design, Nonlinear Architecture, call it what you will, is broadening and deepening its roots and now has many practitioners.[65] The work I will show here is often concerned with an issue close to urban design and Earth Art: that is, how can one handle a large volume of city building without becoming too monumental, clichéd or oppressive in scale? One of the answers is the land-form building, architecture as articulated landscape.

Peter Eisenman's addition to Cincinnati University (see pp139-40) is now complete and a good cxample of the land-form building. It stacks up different activities and spaces onto a pre-existing building, just as one geological formation pushes sediment and rock onto another. The result is part collision – the earthquake of forms that everyone comments on – and part intermeshing of tectonic plates. A new kind of grammar results from these waves of compression, a staccato, clunky, somewhat awkward language which, nevertheless, has its own peculiar grace. Mid-scale volumes, often about the size of a person, weave in and out of each other like a tartan, or shake and tilt against each other like shards after an avalanche. If one decodes the logic behind these stuttering cubes – and Eisenman, like Palladio, invites the user to become involved in the high game of architecture – one can find a color code marking the design process. Light blues, flesh pinks and greens tell you what chunk belongs to what design idea and why it is shifted or tilted or shimmering. The overall result is a new system which, in an unlikely comparison, rcminds one of the Rococo, or the pastel delicacies of Robert Adam. Rococo also shimmers in fractured planes of light, Adamesque architecture has a similar color-tone, but the prettiness and conventionality of both could not have been further from Eisenman's intention.

He seeks to provoke and shock, to decenter perspective, deprivilege any one point of view, cross boundaries, blur categories (especially the boundary between the old stepped building and his new segmental attachment). 'There is no preferred place for the viewer to understand', Eisenman says, invoking the contradictory perspectival space of Piranesi.[66] To achieve these multiple-readings he has adopted several different methods which, characteristically, he has diagrammed clearly, so that aficionados can follow the moves. Chevrons are tilted back and forth off the existing building; they set up one system against which a segmental line – mostly of studio space – is played. This line is 'torqued', 'overlapped' and 'stepped' both as a solid and void. Other moves are made, which I find impossible to understand (could 'phase shift' really be a 'tilt'?). But the result is a relatively new way of generating a sensual architecture.

Inevitably, such a complexity of different formal strategies could only be worked out on a computer and built by using laser technology and a special coordinate system of construction points. Since a team of contractors had to be trained to create this new architecture, it is a pity no film was made during production; if the system is ever repeated, it will have to be reinvented.

One of the most convincing parts of the interior is near the main entrance from the garage side. One comes through a hybrid grid – of window/door/wall – into a symphony of staggered, staccato forms. Overhead, skylights and fluorescent tubes cut up chunks of space; below one's feet, cheap vinyl tile marks the interweaving systems, while the pastel cubes to either side dovetail and layer through each other. These cut-up fragments keep one tense and alert, though the forms make no semantic demand, have no figural message, are completely abstract.

Peter Eisenman, Aronoff Center of Design and Art. *LEFT: Entrance shows self-similar grammar – a new form of weaving. RIGHT: Stair opening onto the atrium – traces of the waves and tilts are picked up in setbacks and the three basic colors. (Photos: Jeff Goldberg, ESTO)*

The lack of representational form (aside from the overall 'earthquake') can be considered a virtue for a modest, infill building, but there is one obvious problem with the whole scheme. Given its high degree of compression (its ceilings and walls pressing in everywhere), given its very deep plan, it cries out for release: for greenery, light from above, a view to the outside from the central atrium. This space, however, in spite of its inwardness, is another one of the small triumphs of the building. Atrium, plaza, square, piazza – the Spanish Steps? None of the prototypes of the public realm are invoked, but all are implied by the way the broad stairway mounts in gentle steps to one side of the triangular 'piazza' below. This is a convivial social space mixing several uses, a public realm which only lacks nature and a symbolic focus.

On a positive level, Eisenman has created a new fabric which is always subtly changing, one in which the architectural drama consists in traces of the design methods pushing through each other – a set of seesawing, blue chevrons marked here versus pink segments there; a tilt to one side, an earthquake to another, and the trapezoidal crush of windows and floors between. It is a new visual language of staccato land-forms and straight tangents that stutter up a hill and around a building; as geology it is more mica than flowing lava, more awkward chunky crystals than the flowing land-forms we will next examine, but nonetheless an important contribution to the idea of the building as complex urban fabric.

Enric Miralles has developed various notation systems for dealing with the land-form building. He depicts the sprawling context of his buildings with a Hockneyesque method of photo-collage; that is, he splices together a continuous image of changing perspectives that wanders in a higgledy-piggledy manner but still keeps a fractal identity, a self-similar quality. Secondly, he has devised what could be called 'cinematic sectioning', the analysis of a large landmass by making many cuts through it. The resulting sections reveal a sequence of varying topography, as if one took cinema stills and flipped through them to animate movement across the land. Cinematic sectioning has been used to depict the complex site of the Eurhythmics Center in Alicante, Spain. Through the notation one follows the rise and fall of land waves as they move under ramps, and the method also choreographs the movement of people on the ramps. From these and other large-scale movements the building is generated. Indeed, the overall undulation of the Center is another fractal, this time one which mimics the surrounding mountains. So the land-form building not only sprawls like a geological formation, it actually miniaturizes one, an idea not far from the way a Chinese garden 'borrows the landscape'.

Cinematic sectioning is a method of controlling the design of very large structures and it was used by several groups who entered the Yokohama Port

Terminal Competition in 1995, an important event for the new paradigm with Greg Lynn, Reiser and Uemoto, and the winners, Foreign Office Architects (FOA), all producing interesting Nonlinear Architecture. The young team of FOA, Farshid Moussavi and Alejandro Zaero-Polo, worked for both Rem Koolhaas and Zaha Hadid and are connected to the Architectural Association in London, with all the apostolic succession this implies. It is no surprise their entry pushes several ideas – folding, superposition and bifurcation – a step beyond their teachers.

Their landscape-building for Japan is a long, low, horizontal, folded plate of steel that will undulate across the water. It gets structural strength from the self-similar folds and the gentle undulations of the plates, flowing forms which are obvious metaphors for the sea. A paradox is that the hard surface resembles a dry desert. It could be a moonscape pock-marked by activities strewn about in a carefully careless way, chaotic compositional tactics that Koolhaas termed 'confetti' when he deployed them at the Parc de la Villette (see p78 for another origin of the land-form building).

The multi-layered topography for Yokohoma achieves both diversity and unity, disjunction and continuity. The architects are looking for a seamless structure, an alternative to collage and radical eclecticism to deal with difference, a system they term 'continuous but not uniform'. They achieve this, to a degree, by folding various functions into a continuous surface full of feedback loops of circulation. If built, the rich mixture of different uses may be hard to administer because the usual visual borders do not orient and divide different kinds of passengers. One can imagine international and local travellers arriving

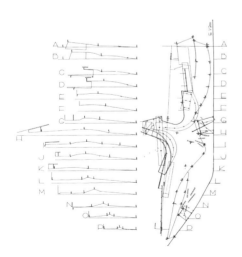

Enric Miralles, Eurhythmics Center, *Alicante, Spain, 1993-94. LEFT: The earth movements under entry ramps spread as wave-forms from A to G and H to P – 'cinematic sectioning'. RIGHT: The rise and fall of the structure in jagged tangents 'borrows the mountainscape'.*

Foreign Office Architects, Yokohama International Port Terminal, *competition winner, 1995.*
The model shows folds in the land-form uniting various activities in a continuous surface
while the cinematic sectioning shows a folded plate in steel – a self-stiffening structure.

175

late for a ship and becoming all mixed up together as they head for one of those eye-shaped folds that peer from one level to the next. These 'bifurcations', as the architects call them, unite different levels in a smooth continuity, rather like origami folds unite a complex pattern into a single sheet of paper.

Opposed to Eisenman's staccato grammar, the grid, the fold and undulation are employed in a soft way that blurs distinctions: one floor warps a bit of itself into another producing a characteristic 'floor/door/window' and a sloping 'floor/ ramp', the latter an idea that Koolhaas has developed. A challenge for architects today is to see if this idea can work better than it does at Frank Lloyd Wright's Guggenheim Museum.

As the model and sections show, this ferry terminal is a very abstract system, a landscape of otherness, a surprising flatscape without the usual orientation points; it does not look like a building at all. The generic nature of the scheme, the architects claim, is well suited to our stage of globalized late-capitalism and, like Mies van der Rohe, they turn a universal system into a kind of transcendental space, a sacred space without a religion. Artificial land, second nature, has reached an apotheosis.

If Foreign Office Architects, this time like Eisenman, prefer an abstract system to a representational one, then the Israeli architect Zvi Hecker reverses the preconception with his Jewish School in Berlin. The Heinz-Galinski School creates an extended land-form out of explicit metaphors. Snake corridors, mountain stairways, fish-shaped rooms are pulled together with an overall sunflower geometry. It sounds constricting, even Procrustean; but on the contrary, the sunflower, with its spiral of movement towards a center, can generate

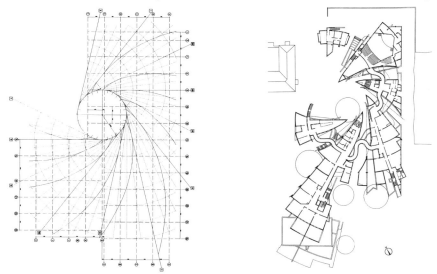

Zvi Hecker, Heinz-Galinski School, Berlin 1993-95. Spiral sunflower geometry (counterclockwise) plus concentric curves plus grid generate complex land-forms and self-similar curves and fish-shapes.

a general order, especially, as here, when tied to two other geometries: those of the grid and concentric circles. The three systems, like Eisenman's tilts, make every room slightly different, or self-similar, and the sunflower spiral results in a very strong pull to the heart of the school (the architect, when he saw it from a helicopter, said it looked like 'a friendly meeting of whales'). Some will find this centrality too obvious, the imagery too readable and insistent, but again one is surprised by the generality and abstraction of the grammar.

This small institution for four hundred and twenty pupils is the first Jewish school to be constructed in Germany for sixty years. Built in the leafy suburbs of Charlottenberg, it literally keeps a low profile – two to three storeys – and threads its sunflower geometry amid the existing trees. The most satisfying aspect is its urbanity. It creates tight curving streets, or walkways, which give a sense of mystery not unlike an historic town, where contingency has created the odd shapes and spaces. Here a restricted palette of grey concrete, silver corrugated metal and white stucco are interwoven with trees. The three colors, as with Eisenman's pink, green and blue, each code a different geometric system. This allows contractors to understand and build a complex woven structure and also, of course, allows the complexity to be read. The point is generally true of these land-form structures. They depend on systematic logic, both for construction and orientation, not the simple logic of one grid, but three or four systems in tandem. Again the contrast with Modern architecture is quite obviously that between complexity and simplicity, although it is not an absolute contrast. Here, for instance, simple materials, simple formulae and abstraction have generated the complexity.

Zvi Hecker, Heinz-Galinski School. *LEFT: An urbanism of tight, curved streets. RIGHT: The central, communal space around which the six forms spin; grey, white and silver materials mark the three generative systems. Note the plan, a concrete punched void, upper right.*

Six of the sunflower petals curve counterclockwise around a circular green and one enters a void where the seventh might have been. This semi-public space, with its subtle mixture of cobbles and grass, metal and stucco, Jewish ruins and concrete, gives a strong sense of identity, the physical counterpart for the strong community life which goes on here. Part Torah school, part synagogue, part community facility with public meeting rooms, the Heinz-Galinski School has to play an ethnic role in Berlin which is not dissimilar to Libeskind's Jewish Museum: it must fit in and yet be unmistakably other.

Several discrete signs, such as a Jewish star, are placed in the background and their presence is felt at the same level as the more purely architectural symbolism; for instance, the plan of the six petals, which is also punched into the concrete. This latter becomes a decorative logo and explanatory map for new visitors. It also suggests the wider intentions of Hecker, which are to produce a cosmic order based on the omnipresent spiral form and, in particular, the solar dynamics of the sunflower. He has underlined the paradox of 'a wild project' that has 'very precise mathematical construction'; 'above all', he notes, 'is its cosmic relationship of spiral orbits, intersecting one another along precise mathematical trajectories.'[67] The mixture of an abstract system and a few discrete signs and images is finely balanced.

The group ARM (Ashton Raggatt McDougall), a Melbourne office, also reaches this balance in some of its post-modern buildings, and the opposition is usually a symbolic programme set against technical virtuosity. At Storey Hall in Melbourne it has created one of the most exuberant expressions of the new paradigm. The building, on one of the main downtown streets of Melbourne, is part of the highly urbanized campus of RMIT. Its explosion of green and purple fractals (with yellow and silver highlights) sends up its neighbors to either side. At the same time, like Gaudi's Casa Batlo with which it is comparable, it also makes subtle acknowledgements to these neighbors, with its cornice line, window scale and basic tripartition. Basically, however, like Eisenman's Cincinnati addition, it is proposing a new urbanism, a new system which is a discrete shift from those of the past, a different way of ordering the landscape which is more organic and chaotic than both the classical and modern systems. Potentially, if it were generalized as a whole street system, it could be just as harmonious as those of the past – a possible new order of urbanism.

At street level, one is confronted by a large green and purple doorway, green folded plates of concrete blur into purple folds (for ARM, like FOA, 'blurring' is a favorite term and here is likened to smeared lipstick). Green and purple were the heraldic colors of previous inhabitants, Irish and feminist groups. In this and other ways, the building takes its cues from history, the typical post-modern method of building in time and historical depth.

Most evident are the patterns of bronze fractals – lozenge shapes, both fat and thin – that dance over the concrete surface. These are versions of the famous Penrose tiling pattern, which I will explain shortly, and they are self-similar to the doorway and other forms in metal: so the variety of shapes are harmonic, related and fractal, but hardly ever self-same (as in a Modernist building).

The bronze panels of the facade are further articulated by a green linear meander, and the surface squiggles look as if they were folds in a rock, or skin. Finally, to the left and on the *piano nobile* (to use the classical term of the adjoining buildings) is a linear part of the Penrose pattern, punched violently through the surface. The architect, Howard Raggatt, ironically quoting one of the responses to the building, speaks of this jagged void as if 'Roger Rabbit went through the concrete wall'; but significantly he sees the point of appropriating the unusual through metaphor and popular culture.[68] He lists the variety and overlap of metaphors – 'broken vegemite jar, kryptonite building, gates of hell, Ivy League creeper, green house for leprechauns, the true geometry of space, from Plato's to Einstein's cave' – suggestive, contrary images which provoke different readings.

Inside the building the variegated themes are elaborated. A high entrance space breaks through several levels, surmounted by a twisting stair, and compressed to one side by the cave entrance. Then one reaches the first-floor foyer whose space is further pushed in by three surfaces – large, abstracted fractals of the facade, folded plates of a bigger dimension. Finally, one reaches the auditorium where the themes are gathered together with even more intensity.

Ashton Raggatt McDougall, Storey Hall, *Melbourne, 1993-96. LEFT: Fractal forms are based on the aperiodic tiling pattern devised by Roger Penrose – a new always-changing order for urbanism. RIGHT: Foyer shows the folded plates compressing in on three sides.*

Ashton Raggatt McDougall, Storey Hall. *Acoustic tile and lighting systems of the auditorium ceiling and wall show aperiodic tiling pattern – and its basic pentagon – at several scales.*

The auditorium ceiling erupts overhead with the Penrose pattern – now in acoustic tile – that is at once reptilian and cave-like. The metaphor of an undulating skin is kept, but developed to accommodate lighting and the requirements of music, drama and lectures. Here, and on the walls and stage, the fractal grammar is played at different scales and in opposite tastes. If Eisenman's system at Cincinnati is abstract, cool but Rococo, ARM's system is representational, hot and Art Deco. At a general level, both architects have used the computer to derive new grammars based on complexity theory, although Storey Hall, because its structure is old, cannot elaborate the grammar in volume.

One of the building's important contributions is its development of the Penrose tiling pattern into an order that connects facade, floor, walls and ceiling into a single ornamental system. Roger Penrose, the Oxford mathematician, inventor and author, discovered a tiling pattern with five-fold symmetry that was previously thought to be impossible. Using a fat and a thin rhombus, he created an aperiodic tiling system which, however far it is extended, never results in a cyclical pattern. Later, in 1984, this unusual, self-organizing order was discovered to exist in nature. It was termed a quasicrystal, because it had an orientational but not translational order, whereas a crystal has both. Like a crystal it has an holistic order, but it also has a higher degree of complexity, since the pattern is everywhere slightly different. Quasicrystals, with a fractal self-similarity, are potentially more suited to architecture than the repetitive use of the square because they are not self-same – or, in a word, boring.

To recognize the Penrose enigma one has to break the pattern down into decagons, which resemble faceted footballs. One begins to discover each football overlaps with another on a thin rhombus. At Storey Hall a more emphatic supergraphic, a green linear pentagon, is laid over the decagons. The two

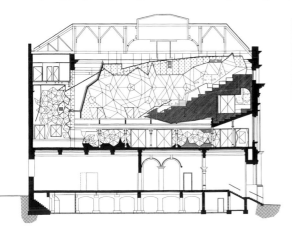

LEFT: ARM, Storey Hall. *Decagons are made from small and large rhombi. RIGHT: Ushida Findlay,* Truss Wall House, *Tokyo, 1994 – a spiral of movement in self-similar curves.*

rhythms then dance together in gentle syncopation, two distinct beats played off against each other. The result may be somewhat overbearing on the street, but in the foyer and auditorium it makes for appropriate, visual music.

Even if they have not answered it, the architects of Storey Hall have posed a very interesting question: What if a whole street were ordered this way? What if a new complexity grammar replaced the self-same rhythms of classicism and Modernism? What if the city grew like a quasicrystal, and an ever-changing order emerged which never quite repeated?

The Japan-based Ushida Findlay Partnership has not quite answered this question either, but also seeks a fractal urban order. This is based on continuous curves, such as the spiral (see p23). The Truss Wall House, Soft and Hairy House, and House for the Millennium are more fluid and continuous than the other buildings illustrated here, because a monotone white surface unites all planes. It absorbs those elements – fixtures and windows – which are usually separated in color and form. Katherine Findlay, who grew up on a Scottish farm, speaks of a fluid, rubbery architecture and, like Eisenman, she favors models such as the slime mould and metaphors taken from movement, because they represent flexibility and activity close to the body.

No architect has yet reached this state of organic flexibility. The Surrealists proposed it in the 1920s and Salvador Dali admired Gaudi's work because it was viscous or, as he called it, 'edible architecture'. Frank Gehry, at the new Guggenheim Museum in Bilbao, approaches this fluidity; he has pushed the grammar he first developed at the Vitra Museum in more supple directions (see pp65-72). At the new Guggenheim, smooth, continuous forms in steel and limestone flow towards a center point to erupt in a flower of petals. Where before at Vitra the units were distorted boxes, now they are more linear, smooth and continuous. The grammar has an all-over, seamless continuity like Ushida Findlay's work.

The building has the presence of a robust, urban plant. It might be a hardy bulb or bush pushing its way opportunistically through holes in the pavement. Tough, riotous, savage – sprouting against the odds, for light and life. It's the image of Gaia overcoming the harsh city hardscape, maybe even a weed thriving on toxic waste. No, it is too graceful for that, but the burgeoning energy is unmistakably present, erupting from below, climbing over the rectilinear structures like a creeper which cannot be suppressed. Actually, many of the gallery spaces are rectilinear – an effective contrast to what happens above – and one of them stretches under the high-speed motorway and bridge to reach up on the other side. This petal serves as another entrance. It also becomes another land-form that ties the building into large-scale technology and the sprawl of the city, urban realities that are accepted not denied by this inclusive work.

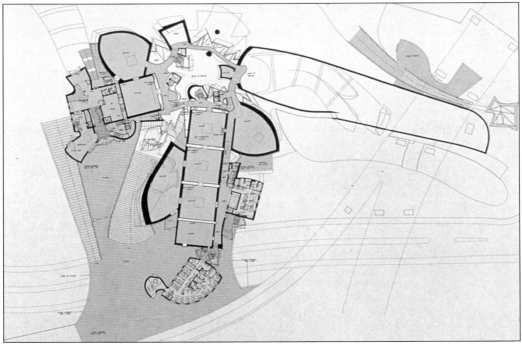

Frank Gehry, The Guggenheim Museum, *Bilbao, Spain, 1993-97. Twenty-six or so self-similar petals erupt in the center and curl under the bridge. In order for the contractors to distinguish petals, they were called 'Cobra', 'Fish', 'Boot', 'Potemkin' and 'Zorro', etc.*

Gehry has related the museum to three city scales: that of the bridge, captured by his tower; that of the existing roof tops, whose heights are acknowledged by the atrium and lower forms; and the Bilbao River, an important historical waterway, which is taken into the scheme, both literally through the large windows and metaphorically through the viscous, silvery forms.

To connect the city to the museum, Gehry has created an atrium space more powerful than any other, even New York's original Guggenheim, which also has a large expanding space at its center (see p157 for an early view of Gehry's model). The Bilbao atrium does not have a function beyond orientation and thus it could be conceived as both a pure aesthetic space and public town square, opening out to the river. Aware that this relative freedom allowed him to upstage Wright at his own game of spatial gymnastics, Gehry said he intends to have a holographic portrait of that wilful architect looking down on visitors, jealously, disapprovingly. Formally, the new atrium takes the exterior grammar and turns it inside out, so that the petal shapes compress inwards, and bend upwards with curved glass. The result is a new kind of ambiguous architecture, more folded onto itself than the glass box which introduced Modernist notions of transparency. Views are partly veiled by walls of light that lead the eye up to the public ramps and roof terraces, which in turn give onto the urban landscape and river – making the museum a celebrant of the city.

While the Bilbao museum has a diversity of form and color, what remains in the mind is the organizing metaphor – the robust flower with its riotous petals blowing in the wind. There are something like twenty-six self-similar petals, which reach out and come to a point extended as a line. Just as a Doric column sculpts light and shadow with its flutes, so these petals are pinched to create a

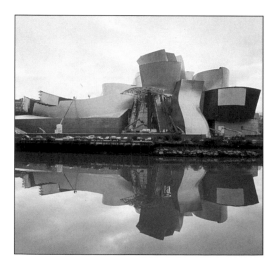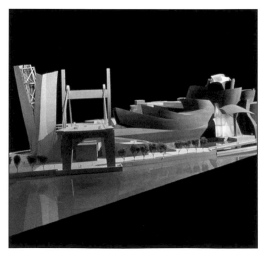

Frank Gehry, The Guggenheim Museum. *Titanium forms pick up the shimmering water.*

shadow line. The arris or fillet defines each volume in a much more subtle way than at Vitra; perhaps this is a visual refinement, but it is also a clear example of the way in which Gehry learns step by step from his own work.

Like so many other buildings in the paradigm, this one has had the fat taken off it by computer. The complex steel framing was kept to a minimum, as was the cutting of the masonry, necessary economies when dealing with curved buildings. There is always a lot of wastage when one carves from a block, unless one can also use the offcuts, or minimize them. Gehry, like Grimshaw and others, has spoken of the way new computer software, designed for other technologies such as aircraft, can be used to cut the cost of fabrication by a large percentage.

The new complexity paradigm in architecture is simultaneously evolving in different directions. The land-form buildings we have looked at constitute just one of the species, perhaps the most prominent, but it does share qualities with the others. Is it the new concern for organic metaphors of design, the petals of Zvi Hecker and Frank Gehry, or the geological formations of Eisenman and Miralles? Is it the attempt to get closer to nature and its fractal language, as ARM and Ushida Findlay are trying to do? Is it the idea of producing an artificial landscape, which they all do to some extent? The overlapping element in common may be the desire to get closer to the reality behind nature, the generative qualities behind both living and dead matter, that is, once again, the cosmogenic process which complexity theory has recently tried to explain. Representing emergence and creativity *per se* cannot be done, but it can be presented by an architecture as fresh and unlikely as one finds here.

The Guggenheim Museum. *Interior atrium, with curved glass walls compressing into the space, showing the pinched arris – which also sculpts strong shadows on the exterior.*

NOTES

1 Ellen Posner, 'Hell's Capital', *The Atlantic Monthly*, July 1994, pp92-99.

2 *Ibid*, pp95, 97.

3 Walter Gropius, proclamation for the exhibit *Arbeitsrat für Kunst*, Berlin, April 1917.

4 Peter Fuller, *Theoria, Art and the Absence of Grace*, Chatto & Windus, London, 1988, p234.

5 *Ibid*, p213.

6 How many terms must one learn? Post-Modernists, not to say postmodernists, are guilty of polluting the world with unnecessary distinctions; but the concept of the post-modern has now stuck and become, *faut de mieux*, the phrase around which the debate on the present and future is conducted. History has chosen this word because it typifies our transitory place of posteriority after Modernity and before a clear alternative has emerged. There are now at least two basic traditions of Post-Modernism, just as there were several of Modernism, and to clarify the 'restructive', 'constructive' or 'ecological' type of this book see my own writings, or that of the following. They constitute, with my wife Maggie and myself, a group called Portrack Seminars: David Ray Griffin has edited about ten anthologies on what he calls 'Constructive Postmodern Thought' brought out by the publisher SUNY, in New York (1988-94, so far); Charlene Spretnak, *States of Grace, The Recovery of Meaning in the Postmodern Age*, (Harper, San Francisco, 1991), and the biologist/philosopher Charles Birch, have developed the notion of 'ecological postmodernism'. Richard Falk, part of our group and professor of International Law at Princeton, has developed a political form of post-modern thought in his several books, to which he has yet to append a prefix. Because of the necessity of distinguishing this tradition from Deconstruction – with which it is sometimes confused in America – we have settled on the uncontaminated 'restructive', which is a combination of 'restructuring' and 'constructive', without the pitfalls of either.

7 Charles Jencks, *What Is Post-Modernism?* Academy Editions, London, St Martin's Press, New York, Third Edition, p43.

8 Robert Venturi, *Complexity and Contradiction*, Museum of Modern Art, New York, Second ed, 1977, p16.

9 'Algorithmic complexity theory', a new branch of mathematics, quantifies the complexity of a sequence of numbers by the length of the shortest computer algorithm that can generate the sequence. The mathematician Charles Bennett of IBM claims it can measure evolutionary complexity, and therefore progress, in terms of DNA information. See Paul Davies, 'Life's Little Complexities', *The Independent*, February 13, 1989, p15. For a discussion applied to literature, see Tito Arecchi, 'Chaos and Complexity', *The Post-Modern Reader*, ed Charles Jencks, Academy Editions/St Martin's, London/New York, 1992, pp350-53. For the related idea of 'Effective Complexity' and 'Algorithmic Information Content' see Murray Gell-Mann, *The Quark and the Jaguar, Adventures in the Simple and the Complex*, Little, Brown and Company, Boston/London, pp34-37, 58-59.

10 Peter Eisenman, who is interested in 'excess', drew my attention to this implication of Coleridge's theory of imagination, especially when it refers to 'more than'.

11 ST Coleridge, *Biographia Literaria*, Chapters XIII, XIV.

12 That life and mind emerge 'at the edge between order and chaos' has been put in different ways by Chris Langton, Stuart Kauffman and others at the Santa Fe Institute. See particularly M Mitchell Waldrop, *Complexity, The Emerging Science at the Edge of Order and Chaos*, Simon and Schuster, New York, 1992, pp198-240, 299-318; and Stuart A Kauffman, *The Origins of Order, Self-Organization and Selection in Evolution*, Oxford University Press, New York, 1993, pp287-341.

13 Paul Davies, *The Cosmic Blueprint*, Simon and Schuster, New York, 1988, p55.

14 'Quantum weirdness' has been an accepted appellation in quantum mechanics for a long time, and even sober and mainstream scientists such as Heinz Pagels use the term as a

matter of course. See his marvellous *The Cosmic Code, Quantum Physics as the Language of Nature*, Bantam, New York, p48 and following. The idea that the mind may have a quantum substrate, or that thought is in part a quantum phenomenon, has been in the air since the 1920s; recent expositions, from different ends of the spectrum, are found in Roger Penrose: *The Emperor's New Mind*, Oxford University Press, New York, London 1989; *Shadows of the Mind, A Search for the Missing Science of Consciousness*, Oxford University Press, New York, London, 1994; and Danah Zohar, *The Quantum Self*, Bloomsbury Publishing, London, 1990.

15 John Briggs & F David Peat, *Turbulent Mirror*, Harper and Row, New York, 1989, p119.

16 Peter Eisenman told me in 1990, when we discussed the idea of a folding in architecture, that he had not heard of David Bohm's important work: see the latter's *Wholeness and the Implicate Order*, Routledge and Kegan Paul, London, 1980; and *The Holographic Paradigm and other Paradoxes*, edited by Ken Wilber, New Science Library, Shambala, Boston, 1985, pp21, 46ff.

17 'Folding in Architecture', *Architectural Design*, 3/4 93, Profile No 102.

18 Ian Stewart, *Does God Play Dice: The Mathematics of Chaos*, Basil Blackwell, Oxford, 1989.

19 Ilya Prigogine and Isabelle Stengers, *Order Out of Chaos, Man's New Dialogue With Nature*, Bantam Books, New York, 1984, pp140-153.

20 Nikolaus Pevsner, 'The Return of Historicism', *Journal of the RIBA*, 3rd series, LXVIII, 1961 and republished in N Pevsner, *Studies in Art, Architecture and Design*, Vol Two, Walker & Co, New York, 1968, pp242-259. This article, attacking what he calls 'outrageous stimulation' (after Wordsworth), has Pevsner's first use of 'post-modern'. He ends it with the rationalist credo: 'If you keep your buildings square, you are not therefore necessarily a square'. True; but to insist on nothing but squares, or primarily squares, is to be an ultra-Modernist with a hang-up.

21 Martin Pawley, 'Fall off Your Chair at the Folly', *The Observer*, May 22, 1994.

22 For a collection of these metaphors see my *Heteropolis, Los Angeles, The Riots and the Strange Beauty of Hetero-Architecture*, Academy/VCH, London, New York, 1993, pp95-100

23 EH Gombrich, 'Visual Metaphors of Value in Art', *Meditations on a Hobby Horse*, Phaidon, London 1963, p12.

24 Translated by David van Zanten, 'Felix Duban and the Buildings of the Ecole des Beaux-Arts, 1832-1840', *Journal of the Society of Architectural Historians*, October 1978, p172, note 35.

25 Peter Eisenman, 'A-Way From/To Architecture', *Anyway*, Anyone Corporation, New York, 1994, p108. Article pp106-115.

26 'Bahram Shirdel, Jeffrey Kipnis', *Space Design 9409*, pp 8-21.

27 M Mitchell Waldrop, *Complexity, The Emerging Science at the Edge of Order and Chaos*, Simon and Schuster, New York, p234.

28 Roger Lewin, *Complexity, Life on the Edge of Chaos*, JM Dent, London, 1993, p51.

29 Niles Eldredge and SJ Gould, 'Punctuated equilibria: an alternative to phyletic gradualism', in TJM Schopf (ed) *Models in Paleobiology*, Freeman, Cooper & Co, San Francisco, 1972, pp82-115.

30 The idea is too omnipresent to need any substantiation, but any of the writings of Richard Dawkins will do. For instance, the point of his *The Blind Watchmaker* (1986) is that the forces of the universe are 'blind'; without *telos*.

31 Paul Davies, *The Cosmic Blueprint*, Simon and Schuster, New York, 1988, pp199-202.

32 'A World Growing Richer', *The Washington Post*, editorial reprinted in *The International Herald Tribune*, June 18, 1994.

33 *Time*, June 27, 1994, p19.

34 EO Wilson, *The Diversity of Life*, Allen Lane, London, 1993, p280.

35 David M Raup, *Extinction, Bad Luck or Bad Genes*, WW Norton & Co, New York, 1991.

36 Julian Simon and Aaron Wildavsky, 'So Biodiversity is Doomed? Let's Take a Cool Recount', *International Herald Tribune*, May 14, 1993, p7.

37 The literature on green architecture is growing fast especially in America and Germany. For a British contribution see the two books by Brenda and Robert Vale: *Towards a Green Architecture*, RIBA Publications, London, 1991 and *Green Architecture, Design for a Sustainable Future*, Thames and Hudson, London, 1991. The work on the architects mentioned has been widely published in architectural magazines.
The World Congress of Architects in Chicago, June 1993 – a combination of the American AIA and UIA – passed 'A Declaration of Interdependence' which committed them to: '1) Place consideration for environment and social sustainability at the core of our design work; 2) Develop innovative practices, procedures, products, services, and standards that will enable us to implement such sustainable design; 3) Educate our fellow professionals, our clients, and the general public about the value and critical importance of sustainable design; 4) Work to change policies, regulations, and standard practices in government and business so that sustainable design will become the fully supported standard practice in the building industry; and 5) work to bring the existing built environment up to sustainable design standards'. One can see by the litany 'sustainable' in every paragraph of this and many politicians' speeches that on paper and on lips we are doing rather well; but the question remains – 'What is sustainability'? How does it relate to the status-quo, foreign trade, inequality, struggle for self-betterment – that is, deep economic issues – as well as time, nationhood and cosmic catastrophes?

38 Mark Swenarton, 'Low Energy Gothic', *Architecture Today* 41, September 1993, p22, report by Dr Peter Rickaby.

39 Imre Makovecz, 'Anthropomorphic Architecture, the Borderline between Heaven and Earth', 'Organic Architecture', *Architectural Design*, 11/12 93, Profile No 106, p15.

40 Marija Gimbutas, *The Language of the Goddess*, Harper, San Francisco, 1989 and *The Civilization of the Goddess, the world of Old Europe*, Harper Collins, New York, 1991.

41 Louise Levathes, 'A Geneticist Maps Ancient Migrations', *New York Times*, July 27, 1993, PP.B 1-B6.

42 Jacques Grinevald, 'A History of the Idea of the Biosphere', in *Gaia, The Thesis, The Mechanism and the Implications*, ed Peter Bunyard and Edward Goldsmith, Wadebridge Ecological Center, 1988, pp1-35.

43 James Lovelock, *Gaia, The Practical Science of Planetary Medicine*, Gaia Books, London, p11.

44 *Ibid*, p11.

45 Edward Goldsmith, 'Ecological Succession Rehabilitated', *The Ecologist*, Vol 15, No3, 1985, pp104-112.

46 *Ibid*.

47 Deyan Sedjic, 'Dazzle and Strife', *The Guardian*, October 19, 1992, p7.

48 Calvin Tomkins, 'Profile on Renzo Piano', *New Yorker*, August 29, p65.

49 Richard Rogers, Interview, September 16, 1994.

50 John Welsh, 'On a Wing and a Layer-Technorganic is the 1990s', *Journal of the RIBA*, July 1994, pp22-29. The interview with John Welsh was on September 14, 1994.

51 There is no single source for this world view, but the concept 'cosmogenesis' is used by the astrophysicist professor David Layzer in Cosmogenesis, *The Growth of Order in the Universe*, Oxford University Press, New York, 1990 and, more generally, by Brian Swimm and Thomas Berry in their *The Universe Story, From the Primordial Flaring Forth to the Ecozoic Era*, Harper, San Francisco, 1992. The writings of Erich Jantsch, Ilya Prigogine, Paul Davies, John Gribbin, Freeman Dyson, James Lovelock, David Bohm, and those mentioned in the Santa Fe Institute have contributed to this paradigm. Like any world view, however, it is much larger than the work of a single corpus of authors.

52 Alan Lightman, *Ancient Light, Our Changing View of the Universe*, Harvard University Press, Cambridge, 1991, p61.

53 Charles Correa, *The Ritualistic Pathway – Five Projects*, AA Publications, London, 1993.

54 Sanford Kwinter, 'The Genius of Matter – Eisenman's Cincinnati Project', *Re-Working Eisenman*, Academy Editions, London, pp91-98.

55 Jacques Derrida, *The Truth in Painting*, translated by Geoff Bennington and Ian McLeod, University of Chicago Press, Chicago, 1987, p25.

56 Pavel Janak, 'From Modern Architecture to Architecture', reprinted in *Czech Cubism*, edited by Alexander von Vegesack, Vitra Design Museum Catalogue, Laurence King/Weil-am-Rhein, 1992.

57 Pavel Janak, 'The Prism and the Pyramid', reprinted in *op cit*.

58 Le Corbusier, *Towards a New Architecture*, London, 1927, pp187, 192.

59 Gunta Stozl in bauhaus archiv, magdalena drost, *bauhaus 1919-1933*, benedikt taschen, Berlin, 1990, p38.

60 Murray Gell-Mann, *The Quark and the Jaguar, Adventures in the Simple and Complex*, Little Brown and Company, London, 1994, pp19-21. See also Stuart A Kauffman, *The Origins of Order, Self-Organization and Selection in Evolution*, *op cit*, Chapter 7, 'The Origins of Life: A New View'.

61 Simon Davies, 'Bionic Man Comes of Age', *The Times*, October 17, 1994.

62 Jay McDaniel, 'The Garden of Eden, the Fall, and Life in Christ: A Christian Approach to Ecology', *Worldviews and Ecology*, edited by Mary Evelyn Tucker and John A Grim, Bucknell University Press, London and Toronto, l993, pp71-82.

63 Hans Christian von Baeyer, *Taming the Atom*, Random House, New York, p162.

64 Paul Davies, *The Mind of God, The Scientific Basis for a Rational World*, Simon and Schuster, New York, 1992, pp82-84.

64 Freeman Dyson, *Infinite in All Directions*, Harper and Row, New York, 1988.

65 The leading practitioners of Cosmogenic Design or Nonlinear Architecture or the Architecture of Emergence are Eisenman, Gehry and, occasionally, Koolhaas and the Organic-Tech architects. Daniel Libeskind and Kisho Kurokawa have buildings in this tradition which are unfinished at the time of writing and are thus not discussed in this second edition. Other examples of Nonlinear Architecture that are in progress are Nicholas Grimshaw's Stock Exchange, Berlin, and Kisho Kurokawa's Fukui City Art Museum. Works that might have been illustrated in a longer discussion include Kijo Rokkaku's Budokan, Tokyo (1990-93), Kathryn Gustafson's gardens in France, Gunter Domenig's Stone House, Austria (1985-95) and perhaps his Z-Bank; Nigel Coates' Penrose Institute, Tokyo (1995), Philip Johnson's Monsta House, New Canaan (1996), the roof structures of Japanese architects Coelecanth, Shoei Yoh, Hitoshi Abe and the sculptural projects of M Takasaki. Also there are the folded plate works of engineers Ted Happold and the Frei Otto group, and the Nonlinear structures of Cecil Balmond; the wooden structures of Herb Greene, Imre Makovecz and Bart Prince; some of Reinma Pietila's work, especially the early Dipoli Centre and Kiillemoreeni. Important theorists and designers who are developing the paradigm include Jeff Kipnis, Greg Lynn, Bahram Shirdel, Reiser Umemoto and Ben van Berkel. A very early work to explore the form language of folding and curves is Frederick Kiesler's Endless House (1959), developed from his Endless Theatre of 1926.

66 Peter Eisenman quoted in Joseph Giovannini, 'Campus Complexity', *Architecture*, AIA Journal, Washington, DC, August 1996, pp114-25.

67 Zvi Hecker quoted in pamphlet *Heinz-Galinski-Schule Berlin*, Aedes Galerie und Architektur-forum, January 1993, p14.

68 Howard Raggatt and ARM, 'New Patronage', from pamphlet *RMIT Storey Hall*, Faculty of Environmental Design, RMIT, Melbourne, 1996, pp8-9

INDEX